CHINESE STUDIES
A BIBLIOGRAPHIC MANUAL

Chinese Materials Center, Inc.
Bibliographic Series No. 1

Chinese Studies
A Bibliographic Manual

by

Ernst Wolff

With the Assistance of
Maureen Corcoran

Chinese Materials Center, Inc.
San Francisco
1981

ISBN 0-89644-627-1

PRINTED IN THE REPUBLIC OF CHINA

Contents

Preface

Several of my colleagues have asked me for copies of the notes that I have accumulated over my years of teaching Chinese bibliography and reference. Since there are few guides for such a course, I have decided to publish my notes in the form of a manual to be supplemented in class by the knowledge of a competent teacher. Explanatory text and duplication of existing research tools, such as Teng and Biggerstaff, are therefore kept to a minimum. However, it is hoped that the basic tools, topics, and problems of Chinese bibliography, or Chinese research methodology, as some prefer to call it, will become apparent and that this manual will prove useful to all who approach the subject–beginners, experienced China scholars, and expecially teachers. Librarians not acquainted with Chinese reference materials and bibliography may also find this manual useful as an introduction to the problems of East Asian research.

The conversion of my random notes to systematic form in a manual would not have been possible without the constructive criticism and active contributions of Ms. Maureen Corcoran, to whom much credit is due.

ERNST WOLFF

Abbreviations

AAS	Association for Asian Studies
BEFEO	*Bulletin de l'Ecole Francaise d'Extreme-Orient*, Paris.
Berton and Wu Guide	*Contemporary China; a Research Guide.* Peter Berton and Eugene Wu. Stanford, Calif., Hoover Institution, 1967.
BMFEA	*Bulletin of the Museum of Far Eastern Antiquities*, Stockholm
HJAS	*Harvard Journal of Asiatic Studies*
JAOS	*Journal of the American Oriental Society*
JAS	*Journal of Asian Studies*
LJ	*Library Journal*
MCBRAS	*Journal of the North China Branch of the Royal Asiatic Society*

SKTY	*Ssu-k'u ch'üan-shu tsung-mu t'i-yao* 四庫全書總目提要
SPPY	*Ssu-pu pei-yao* 四部備要
SPTK	*Ssu-pu ts'ung-k'an* 四部叢刊
Teng and Biggerstaff	*An Annotated Bibliography of Selected Chinese Reference Works.* 3rd rev. edition. Teng Ssu-yü and Knight Biggerstaff. Cambridge, Mass., Harvard Univ. Pr., 1971.
TPKC	*T'ai-p'ing kuang-chi* 太平廣記
TPYL	*T'ai-p'ing-yü-lan* 太平御覽
TSCC	*Ts'ung-shu chi-ch'eng* 叢書集成

A newsletter promoting increased attention to Asian studies in elementary and secondary education.

A 3. *China Exchange Newsletter.* Committee on Scholarly Communications with the People's Republic of China, Washington, D.C., 1973-.
Usually contains a bibliography of most recent publications on the mainland.

A 4. *Asia Documentation Service Acquisitions of the Library.* Documentation Service, Institute of Asian Affairs, Hamburg, Germany, 1973-.

A 5. *Bulletin* (formerly *Newsletter*) *of the Committee on East Asian Libraries.* Committee on East Asian Libraries, Association for Asian Studies, Ann Arbor, Michigan, 53-:1977-.

And finally, to set the mood and point to some of the problems and the general scope of our endeavor, the following readings are recommended:

A 6. "Methods in Sinology." Elling Eide in *JAS* 31.1:131-41 (November 1971).

A 7. "Recent Developments in Chinese Studies." L. Carrington Goodrich in *JAOS* 85.2:117-21 (April-June 1965).

B. General Bibliographies on Asia and China

This section lists reference works with a broad scope designed to give a survey of the field. There are many such works relevant to Chinese studies of which the following are only a highly selective few. When considering the use of these works, the student is reminded to note the publication date as a clue to interpreting its applicability to specific bibliographic needs.

B 1. "China," in *A World Bibliography of Bibliographies, 1964-1974.* Alice F. Toomey. Totowa, N.J: Rowman, 1977. 2 vols.
The "China" section is in volume 1, pp. 205-16. It lists a good selection of up to date bibliographies in the "Besterman" tradition.

B 2. *Oriental and Asian Bibliography: An Introduction with Some References to Africa.* James Douglas Pearson. Hamden, Conn.: Archon Books, 1966.
A descriptive treatment of the field with much material on and about Asian studies and resources. Note in particular chapter 2 on the history of Asian studies in various countries and chapter 4 on organizations interested in Asian studies.

B 3. *Asia: A Selected and Annotated Guide to Reference Works.* Godfrey Raymond Nunn. Cambridge, Mass.: MIT Press, 1971.
"Clear and accurate annotations . . . unerring sense of selection." Review in *JAS* 31:2:470 (February 1972).

B 4. *Asian Resources in American Libraries.* Teresa S. Yang, Thomas C. Kuo, Frank Joseph Shulman. New York: Paragon, 1977.
Discusses the history of Asian resources in the United States. Provides "a bibliographical guide to East Asian resources in American libraries"; see pp. 49-142.

B 5. *Books on Asia from the Near East to the Far East: A Guide for the General Reader, Selected and Annotated.* Eleazar Birnbaum. Toronto: University of Toronto Press, 1971.
A highly selective listing of important books on China with short annotations. The China section (pp. 209-46) has about 250 entries.

B 6. *Northeastern Asia: A Selected Bibliography.* Robert Joseph Kerner. Berkeley: University of California Press, 1939. 2 vols.
Lists 13,884 items in 7 major languages. Useful for the volume of entries alone. Criticized for omitting important works; see L. K. Rosinger in *Pacific Affairs* 13:111-13 (1940).

B 7. *East Asia: A Bibliography of Bibliographies.* Godfrey Raymond Nunn. Honolulu: East-West Center, 1967.
The introduction is dated February 1967. Its China section (29 pages) lists basic bibliographies with one location in the United States given for each.

B 8. *China: A Resources and Curriculum Guide.* Arlene Posner and Arne J. de Keijzer. 2nd rev. ed. Chicago: University of Chicago Press, 1976.
A guide to help elementary and secondary teachers "develop a meaningful program" on China; see p. xv. Includes nonbook material. Useful for the general reader.

B 9. *China: Selected Readings.* Hyman Kublin. 2nd ed. Boston: Houghton Mifflin, 1972.
A good selection for the general reader.

B 10. *Modern China.* Richard Harris. 2nd ed. London: National Book League, 1965.
Too old for some topics, but presents a good selection for the period 1840 to 1949.

B 11. "Sixty Good Books on China." Charles W. Hayford and Andrew J. Nathan, in *LJ* 97.2:2341-47 (July 1972).
This and item [B 12] are excellent selections of contemporary material on China.

B 12. "China in Print: Current Travel, History and Descriptive Books." Dorothy Scott, in *LJ* 97.29:3769-74 (November 1972).

B 13. *Asia: A Core Collection.* Godfrey Raymond Nunn. Ann Arbor, Mich.: Xerox University Microfilms, 1973.
Selection by experts of 1000 books in English appropriate for college use. Reference works, periodicals and periodical articles are not included. There are 241 books on China (pp. 42-62).

B 14. *A Union List of Selected Western Books on China in American Libraries.* Charles Sydney Gardner, comp. 2nd ed., rev. and enl. New York: Burt Franklin, 1970.

B 15. *Chinese Collections in the Library of Congress: Excerpts from the Annual Reports of the Librarian of Congress, 1898-1971.* Ping-kuen Yu 余秉權. Center for Chinese Research Materials, Association for Research Libraries, Washington, D. C., 1974.
This reproduces the section on China in the Librarian of Congress annual reports and gives interesting write-ups on various works of Chinese literature.

C. Basic Reference Works on China

The books listed in this section are more comprehensive than those of the preceding section. They are the essential Western language reference works on China. I have divided them into two groups. The first group consists of the "front line" of reference works that no reference collection on China can afford to be without. The second group lists strong supplements to that core. The student should read all introductory material in the works themselves, as well as the cited reviews.

CORE GROUP

C 1. *Bibliotheca Sinica: Dictionnaire bibliographique des ouvrages relatifs a l'Empire Chinois.* Henri Cordier. Paris: Guilmoto; Guethner, 1904-1924. 5 vols. Repr 1.
A comprehensive bibliography of all Western writings on China from the earliest Western contacts with China until about 1924, by one of the greatest pioneers of Western sinology; see the eulogy by Paul Pelliot in *T'oung Pao* 24:1-15 (1926). Columbia University compiled the author index, which is added to volume 5 in the reprint edition.

C 2. *China in Western Literature.* Yuan Tung-li, comp. New Haven, Conn.: Far Eastern Publishers, Yale University, 1958.
A continuation of Cordier's *Bibliotheca Sinica,* the work's foreword promises "a record of virtually all books concerning China published in English, French and German between 1921 and 1957." Reviewed by R. Loewenthal in *JAS* 18:500-1 (1958-59), and by G. E. Sargent in *Journal of Oriental Studies* (Hongkong) 5.1-2:223-27

(1959-60). Sargent's article includes a bibliography of earlier related works.

C 3. *Index Sinicus.* John Lust with the assistance of Werner Eichhorn. Cambridge, Eng.: Heffner, 1964.
A catalog of articles in western languages relating to China appearing in periodicals and other collective publications, 1920-1955. Intended to supplement the *Bibliotheca Sinica* and *China in Western Literature.* Its publication was praised as "an event of major importance" by Edwin G. Beal in his review in *JAS* 24:691-92 (1965).

C 4. *China: A Critical Bibliography.* Charles O. Hucker. Tucson: University of Arizona Press, 1962.
A selected, graded, and annotated list of books, articles, and individual chapters that contribute significantly to the study of China. Well organized with helpful introductory notes and concise, illuminating annotations.

C 5. *Bibliography of Asian Studies.* Association for Asian Studies. Ann Arbor, Mich. Annual. Cumulated by G. K. Hall, Boston, Mass., in two volumes covering the periods 1941-1965 and 1966-1970.
An extensive bibliography of books and periodical articles. Read "Origin and Development of the *Bibliography of Asian Studies*" by E. H. Pritchard in *Library Resources on East Asia* (Zug, Switzerland: Interdocumentation, 1968), pp. 9-13.

C 6. *Contemporary China: A Research Guide.* Peter Berton and Eugene Wu. Stanford, Calif.: Hoover Institution, 1967.
Limited to post-1949 Mainland China and post-1945 Taiwan. Reviewed by Franklin W. Houn in *JAS* 28:153-55 (1968). Usually referred to as the "Berton and Wu Guide."

C 7. *Modern China, 1840-1872: An Introduction to Sources and Research Aids.* Andrew J. Nathan. University of Michigan, Center for Asian Studies, 1973.
Aimed at the American graduate student in history or the

social sciences. Excellent selections in short space (95 pages). Reviewed by Jane L. Price in *JAS* 33:309-10 (1974).

C 8. *The History of Imperial China: A Research Guide.* Endymion Wilkinson. Cambridge, Mass.: Harvard University Press, 1973.
Broad coverage of primary sources and an introduction to the research aids in Chinese, Japanese, and western languages that facilitate use of these sources. Reviewed by N. Sivin in *JAS* 34:821-24 (1975).

C 9. *Modern Chinese Society: An Analytical Bibliography.* George William Skinner, ed. Stanford: Stanford University Press, 1973. 3 vols.
An indispensable aid in studying contemporary Chinese society—but note its limited structure-of-society approach: the more sociocultural topics are omitted. It also omits international relations and the situation of the overseas Chinese. Nevertheless, every student should be familiar with this work. The following reviews are recommended: Mark Elvin and Piet van der Loon in *China Quarterly* 59:587-92 (July-September 1974); and the "Review Symposium" in *JAS* 35.2:277-99 (February 1976) (especially the sections by Edwin G. Beal and Andres J. Nathan).

SUPPLEMENTARY GROUP

C 10. *Revue Bibliographique de Sinologie.* Ecole des Hautes Etudes en Sciences Sociales. Paris: Mouton, 1957-.
Starts with 1955 publications in English and French. Cooperative reviews that are descriptive, rather than critical, by specialists (mainly European). Covers articles and books in the humanities and social sciences written mainly in Western languages. Some selected Russian, Japanese and Chinese works are included. Read the introduction to the first volume. Unfortunately, there

is a long delay between a work's publication date and its review in this work (volume 11, covering 1965, was published in 1977).

C 11. *Annual Bibliography of Oriental Studies.* 東洋學文獻類目. (Tōyōgaku bunken ruimoku). Research Institute for Humanistic Studies, Kyoto University, 1935.
A listing, without annotations, of works written in East Asian and Western languages. Strong in Chinese classical studies. Delay of about two years between a work's publication date and its listing in this bibliography.

C 12. *The Chinese Reader's Manual: A Handbook of Biographical, Mythological and General Literary Reference.* William Frederick Mayers. Shanghai: American Presbyterian Mission Press, 1874. Repr 1.
Primarily a biographical dictionary, but includes mythical and legendary characters. Part II is noteworthy for its listing of symbolic numerical categories.

C 13. *Notes on Chinese Literature.* Alexander Wylie. Shanghai: American Presbyterian Mission Press, 1867. Repr 1.
A comprehensive survey of Chinese classical literature with easy reference guides. Read: W. Mayers, "In memoriam; Alexander Wylie," *NCBRAS* 21:305-8 (1886); Howard S. Levy, "Preface to the second edition," 1963; review by Liu Chun-jo, JAS 24.2:328-9 (February 1963).

C 14. *The Encyclopaedia Sinica.* Samuel Couling. Shanghai: Kelly and Walsh, 1917. Repr 1.
Only 633 pages but useful for quick, short answers to basic questions. Originally designed as a source of information for readers interested in China during the treaty-port days.

C 15. *China: A Handbook.* Wu Yuan-li, ed. New York: Praeger, 1973.
Contains articles by different China specialists on various aspects of China. Described in its preface as "a reference book on Mainland China (i.e. the PRC) for the general readership."

C 16. *The People's Republic of China, a Handbook.* Harold C. Hinton, ed. Boulder, Colo.: Westriew Press, 1979.
Presents essays by experts on various aspects of today's China.

For readers of German, there are three more valuable works:

C 17. *China-Handbuch.* Wolfgang Franke, ed. Duesseldorf: Bertelsman, 1974.
Encyclopedic arrangement of articles written by various specialists. Readers with no knowledge of German may also benefit from the bibliographic notes at the end of each article.

C 18. *Bücherkunde zur chinesischen Geschichte, Kultur und Gesellschaft.* Rainer Hoffmann. Munich, Germany: Weltforum, 1953.
A comprehensive, well annotated bibliography. A particularly welcome feature is the listing of review articles on the various works cited in this bibliography.

C 19. *Sinologie.* Herbert Franke. Bern: A. Francke, 1953.
Out of date now in many respects, but a very readable bibliographic introduction to sinology.

For readers of Russian, the following should also be of interest:

C 20. *Bibliografiia Kitaia* (Chinese bibliography). Moscow: P. E. Skachkov, 1960.
A bibliography of the major Russian-language publications from 1730 to 1957 on all phases of Chinese history and culture.

C 21. *Istoriko-bibliograficheskii obzor istochnikov . . . istorii Kitaia.* G. V. Efimov. Leningrad, 1965-1972. 3 vols.
A survey of Russian sources on modern Chinese history.

C 22. "An Introductory Note on Soviet Sources on Contemporary China." Paul H. Borsuk. *Center for Chinese Research Materials Newsletter* (Washington, D.C.) 18:3-5 (June 1975).

C 23. "Russian Sources." C. Kiriloff, in *Essays on the Sources for Chinese History.* Columbia, South Carolina: University of South Carolina Press, 1975, pp. 188-202.

C 24. *Russian Studies on China: Progress and Problems of Soviet Sinology.* E. Stuart Kirby. Totowa, N. J.: Rowman and Littlefield, 1976.

C 25. *New Books on Asia Announced for Publication in the Soviet Union.* William L. MacDonald. Center for Asian Studies, University of Illinois. Urbana, Illinois, 1972-. Irregularly published. Selections translated into English from *Bibliografia vostoka* (published by the Soviet Academy of Sciences).

D. Chinese Bibliography Proper

This somewhat facile approach through chiefly Western language materials on Western sources may have imparted a false sense of ease and manageability. However, we now approach the more awesome part of our endeavor—the Chinese bibliography proper. These are the bibliographic aids, for the most part in Chinese, designed to guide the researcher through the voluminous Chinese literature.

For the reader who is relatively unfamiliar with Chinese bibliography three introductory readings are recommended:

D 1. "History of Bibliographic Classification in China." Tsien Tsuen-hsuin, in *Library Quarterly* 22:307-24 (1952). Highlights the main concerns of Chinese librarians over the centuries of bibliographic development in China.

D 2. *Chinese Traditional Historiography*. Charles S. Gardner. Cambridge, Mass.: Harvard University Press, 1961 (First published in 1938).
Scan this work for the core problems of Chinese bibliography in general, such as formal classification (chapter VII) and textual criticism (chapter III).

D 3. *Histoire de la Bibliographie Chinoise.* Woo Kang 吳康. Paris: Leroux, 1938.
This appears to be the only truly comprehensive study of Chinese historical bibliography. Note that it gives merely an outline of Chinese schemes of classification and library structure up to 1938, rather than guidance on the usefulness and how to use the various reference books mentioned.

The works listed above concern themselves with the Chinese traditional libraries and library techniques. Modern librarianship in China may be said to have been promoted mainly through American influences. Read:

D 4. "Miss Mary Elizabeth Wood: Pioneer of the Library Movement in China." George W. Huang 黄文宏, in *Journal of Library and Information Science* 1.1:67-68 (April 1975).

D 5. "Modern Library Movement in China." A. Kaiming Chiu, in *Libraries in China* (Papers prepared on the occasion of the 10th anniversary of the Library Association of China). Peiping, 1935, pp. 1-17.

As a result of these influences Chinese librarians in the thirties produced two bibliographies of Chinese reference works modelled after Western examples, namely:

D 6. *Chung-wen ts'an-k'ao-shu chih-nan* 中文參考書指南. Ho To-yüan 何多源. Ch'ang-sha: Commercial Press, 1938; Taipei Repr: Wen-shih-che, 1970.

D 7. *Chung-wen ts'an-k'ao-shu chü-yao* 中文參考書舉要. Teng Yen-lin 鄧衍林. Peking: National Library of Peking, 1936; Taipei Repr: Ku-t'ing, 1969.

Both these bibliographies have by now lost most of their practical usefulness, since they have been superceded by the following publication:

D 8. *An Annotated Bibliography of Selected Chinese Reference Works.* Teng Ssu-yü 鄧嗣禹 and Knight Biggerstaff. 3rd rev. ed. Cambridge, Mass.: Harvard University Press, 1971. Provides "Western students in the field of Sinology with an elementary guide to the most important Chinese reference works. A few of the best editions available are listed under each title, followed by a note briefly describing the contents of the work or giving directions regarding its use." (Preface to the first edition). From now on I shall refer to this primary aid merely as "Teng and Biggerstaff."

In addition there are three later Taiwan publications which supplement Teng and Biggerstaff to some extent, and are particularly valuable for information on Taiwan reprints of earlier, previously out-of-print, Chinese reference works:

D 9. *Chung-wen ts'an-k'ao yung-shu chih-nan* 中文參考用書指南. Li Tze-chung 李志鍾 and Wang Yin-lan 汪引蘭. Taipei: Cheng-chung, 1972.
Reviewed by Robert Chen 陳品金 in *Journal of Library and Information Science* 1.1:115-6 (April 1975).

D 10. *Chung-wen kung-chü-shu chih-yin* 中文工具書指引. Ying Yü-k'ang 應裕康 and Hsieh Yün-fei 謝雲飛. Taipei: Lantai, 1974.

D 11. *Chung-wen ts'an-k'ao yung-shu chiang-i* 中文參考用書講義. Chang Chin-lang 張錦郎. Taipei: Wen-shih-che, 1976.
While the first two works, [D 9] and [D 10], are more or less lists with short annotations (note their informative prefaces), the last one, [D 11], consists of essay-style introductions to the various sections of Chinese bibliography.

HISTORY OF PRINTING AND BOOK CLASSIFICATION IN CHINA

A history of books begins with the history of writing and reproduction. The art of printing was first effectively practiced in China. An understanding of its history will provide the student with some perspective on the nature of the written record.

Suggested reading:

D 12. "Chinese printing." Ernst Wolff, in *Encyclopedia of Library and Information Science.* New York: Marcel Dekker. Vol 24 (1978) 76-87.

A short résumé of the subject, with a highly selective bibliography at the end of the article.

D 13. *The Invention of Printing in China and its Spread Westward.* Thomas Francis Carter. 2nd ed. revised by L. C. Goodrich. New York: Ronald Press, 1955.
The classic Western source on printing in East Asia. Although some of its information may require updating in the face of more recent archeological finds, it is still an invaluable source book.

D 14. *Written on Bamboo and Silk: The Beginning of the Chinese Books and Inscriptions.* Tsien Tsuen-hsuin. Chicago: University of Chicago Press, 1962.
A readable account of the history of Chinese inscriptions on stones, bronzes, jade, mirrors, seals, coins and pottery. Richly illustrated.

D 15. *Chung-kuo yin-shua-shu ti fa-ming chi ch'i ying-hsiang.* 中國印刷術的發明及其影響. Chang Hsiu-min 張秀民. Peking: Jen-min, 1958.
A work in Chinese comparable to Carter's, [D 13], but with greater detail regarding Chinese sources and more recent archeological finds.

The collection and preservation of documents and records goes even further back in Chinese history than the invention of paper, printing and book-making. However, many of the archival treasures of China's antiquity have been destroyed in the course of history through natural and man-made calamities. Particularly noteworthy events in this respect were: (1) The infamous book-burning by Ch'in-shih-huang-ti in 213 B.C.; and (2) Hsiang Yü's destruction of the imperial library after he captured the capital, Hsien-yang, in 206 B.C.

Suggested reading:

D 16. *Ku-chin tien-chi chü-san k'ao* 古今典籍聚散考. Ch'en Teng-yüan 陳登原. Shanghai: Commercial Press, 1936. Reprinted in Taiwan.

The early emperors of the Han dynasty (206 B.C.-220 A.D.) are credited with efforts to rebuild the imperial library by systematic collection of books throughout the empire, described in chapter 30 of Pan Ku's *Han-shu* in the following words:

> 漢興改秦之敗大收篇籍廣開獻書之路. (When the Han came to power, they amended the faults of the Ch'in. They collected written records on a wide scale and opened wide the way for book donations.)

As the imperial library grew to certain dimensions, it was only natural that its custodian should compile a library catalog. The first such catalog of which we have knowledge was initiated by Liu Hsiang 劉向 (80 B.C. to 9 B.C.) and completed by his son Liu Hsin 劉歆 (1st cent. B.C. and A.D.). The original has been lost but it is generally assumed that when Pan Ku compiled his *Han-shu*, he incorporated the booklist of the Lius and their book classification scheme in the *"I-wen chih"* 藝文志 (Essay on Literature), chapter 30 of his *Han-shu.*

Suggested readings:

D 17. "Concerning the importance of the I-wen-chih." E. R. Hughes, in *Mélanges chinoises et bouddhiques* 6:173-82 (1938/39).

D 18. *Chung-kuo mu-lu-hsüeh tzu-liao hsüan-chi* 中國目錄學資料選輯. Ch'ang Pi-te 昌彼得. Taipei: Wen-shih-che, 1972.

The *Han-shu i-wen-chih* 漢書藝文志 divides its booklist into seven groups, the *ch'i-lüeh* 七略 (Seven outlines), with further subdivisions in each group, as circumstances demand. The seven main groups are:

1. Generalia 輯略
2. The Six Classics 六藝略
3. Philosophers of Various Schools 諸子略
4. *Shih* and *fu* poetry 詩賦略

5. Military Science兵書略
6. Astronomy/Divination術數略
7. Medicine and Pharmacopeia方技略

Suggested readings on the *ch'i-lüeh* system:

D 19. "Beginning of Library Cataloging in China." Chiang Fu-ts'ung, in *Chinese Culture* 8:144-58 (December 1967).

D 20. "Historical Development of Classification Systems in China." K. T. Wu, in *Libraries in China* (Papers prepared on the occasion of the 10th anniversary of the Library Association of China). Peiping, 1935, pp. 20-3.

Additional readings:

D 21. "Han-shu i-wen-chih." Teng and Biggerstaff, pp. 7-8.

D 22. "The Authority of the Chinese Classics." James Legge, in his "Prolegomena" to *The Chinese Classics.* Oxford: Clarendon Press, 1893-95; repr: Hongkong University Press, 1960, vol. 1, pp. 3-11.

D 23. *Pan Piao, Pan Ku and the Han History.* Otto P. N. B. Van der Sprenkel. Centre of Oriental Studies, Australian National University, Canberra, 1964.

D 24. *Chinese Traditional Historiography* [D 2], pp. 32-38.

D 25. *Histoire de la bibliographie chinoise* [D 3], pp. 2-4: "Introduction."

D 26. *Chung-kuo mu-lu-hsüeh shih* 中國目錄學史. Hsü Shih-ying 許世英. Taipei: Chung-hua, 1954.

D 27. "Lun ch'i-lüeh tsai wo kuo mu-lu-hsüeh shih shang ti ch'eng-chiu ho ying-hsiang" 論七略在我國目錄學史上的成就和影響. Wang Chung-min 王重民, in *Li-shih yen-chiu* 歷史研究 no. 4:177-90 (1963).

The *ch'i-lüeh* system remained the standard classification scheme until a certain Hsün Hsü 荀勗 (d. 289 A.D.) of the Chin 晉 dynasty compiled a booklist, the *Chung-ching* 中經 (Important Books of the Inner Palace), in which he used four main divisions. He marked the four divisions merely by the first cyclical numbers 甲乙丙丁 –equivalent roughly to our a-b-c-d. Each of these main divisions was then subdivided as is the still extant *Sui-shu ching-chi chih* 隋書經籍志 (see below).

Suggested reading:

D 28. *Chung-kuo shih-pu mu-lu hsüeh* 中國史部目錄學. Cheng Ho-sheng 鄭鶴聲. Taipei: Commercial Press, 1966, pp. 9-11.

D 29. "Chung-ching hsin pu" 中經新溥. T. Morohashi, in *Dai Kanwa Jiten* [E 51], vol. 1, p. 295.

Although the *Chung-ching* in its original form is no longer extant, Wei Cheng 魏徵 (580-643) applied the four-division classification when he compiled the book catalog of the Sui dynasty, the *Sui-shu ching-chi chih*, which is extant. This classification system gained gradual acceptance and in modern times was used in the catalogue of the K'ang-hsi's Emperor library in Peking, the *Ssu-k'u ch'üan-shu tsung-mu* 四庫全書總目 [G 4]. The system was hence called the *ssu-pu* 四部 (four departments) or *ssu-k'u* 四庫 (four treasuries, i.e., four sections of the imperial library) system of classification. The four divisions were designated as *ching, tzu, shih, chi* 經子史集 (classics, philosophers, history, belles lettres). For a chart of the complete system, and an example of a modern application, see:

D 30. *Kyōto Daigaku Jimbun Kagaku Kenkyujō kanseki bunrui mokuroku* 京都大學人文科學研究所漢籍分類目錄. Research Institute for Humanistic Studies, Kyoto University, 1963-1965. 2 volumes. See vol 1, pp. 1-6.

THE FORTY-FOUR SUBDIVISIONS OF THE SSU-K'U CH'ÜAN-SHU

(English translations are those of Taam Cheuk-woon [G 3])

經	CLASSICS
易	Book of Changes
書	Book of History
詩	Book of Poetry
禮	Rituals
春秋	Spring and Autumn Annals
孝經	Book of Filial Piety
五經總義	Commentaries on the Classics
四書	The Four Books
樂	Music
小學	Dictionaries
史	HISTORY
正史	Official Histories
編年	Annals
紀事本末	Complete Records
別史	Unofficial Histories
雜史	Miscellaneous Histories
詔令奏議	Edicts, Petitions, etc.
傳記	Biographies
史鈔	Historical Excerpts
載記	Annals of the Independent States
時令	Chronography, Books on the Seasons, etc.
地理	Geography and Topography
職官	Official Registers
政書	Administration, Jurisprudence, Economics, etc.
目錄	Bibliographies
史評	Historical Critiques

子 PHILOSOPHY

儒家	Writers on Confucianism
兵家	Writers on Military Science
法家	Writers on Law
農家	Writers on Agriculture
醫家	Writers on Medicine
天文算法	Astronomy and Mathematics
術數	Divination
藝術	Arts
譜錄	Repertories of Science
雜家	Miscellaneous Writers
類書	Encyclopedias
小說	Essays and Tales
釋家	Buddhism
道家	Taoism

集 BELLES-LETTRES

楚辭	Elegies of Ch'u
別集	Individual Collections
總集	General Collections
詩文評	Critiques on Poetry and Prose
詞典	Poetical Compositions and Songs

CHINESE BIBLIOGRAPHIC TERMINOLOGY

During the centuries since the inception of printing and book-making in China, the Chinese have evolved a technical terminology, particularly with regard to the peculiarities of the Chinese book in its traditional form, e.g., its thread-bound fascicles (*ts'e* 冊), of which 4, 6, or more are usually placed into a case (*t'ao* 套), etc. English glossaries to these technical terms may be found in:

D 31. "Bibliographic terms." A. C. Moule, in *New China Review* 3.4:254-8 (August 1921).

D 32. *Chinese Popular Fiction.* Liu Tsun-yan. Hongkong: Lung-men, 1967; especially pp. 8-12.

D 33. *Elementary Chinese for American Librarians: A Simple Manual.* John T. Ma. Hanover, N. H.: Oriental Society, 1968; especially pp. 11-24.

D 34. *Ku-chi pan-pen ch'ien-shuo* 古籍版本淺說. Ch'en Kuo-ch'ing 陳國慶. Shengyang: Liao-ning jen-min, 1957.
This is an unpretentious but useful ninety-six-page work. Note in particular the index of terms on pp. 92-6. Other chapters deal with imprint terms, e.g., block print, movable type print (pp. 18-48); printing style, layout, type, illustrations (pp. 49-65); the evolution of Chinese book binding (pp. 66-81).

D 35. "Pan-pen ming ch'eng shih lüeh" 版本名稱釋略. Li Wen-ch'i 李文裿, in *Chung-kuo shu-chi yen-pien lun chi* 中國書籍演變論集. Hongkong: Chung-kuo t'u-shu-kung-ssu, 1972, pp. 51-71.

D 36. "Chung-kuo shu-chi chuang-ting chih pien-ch'ien" 中國書籍裝釘之變遷. Li Wen-ch'i 李文裿, in *Chung-kuo shu-chi yen-pien lun chi*, pp. 165-176.

With the advent of Western book-making technology and library administration, new terms were coined in these fields. The Chinese frequently followed earlier Japanese usage of the pertinent terminology. It is therefore important to list here the first two Japanese dictionaries of modern library terms:

D 37. *Toshokangaku shoshigaku jiten* 圖書館學書誌學辭典 ("Dictionary of Librarianship and Bibliographical Terms"). Uemura Chōzaburō 植村長三郎. Tokyo: Yurindo, 1972.

D 38. *Shuppan jiten* 出版事典. Tokyo: Shuppan Nyusu Sha, 1971.

Some Chinese dictionaries and glossaries of modern library terms:

D 39. *T'u-shu-kuan-hsüeh tz'u-tien* 圖書館學辭典. Lu Chen-ching 盧震京. Peking: Commercial Press, 1958.

D 40. *T'u-shu-kuan-hsüeh shu-yü chien-shih* 圖書館學術語簡釋 ("Glossary of Library Terms"). Wang Cheng 王征. T'ai-chung: Wen-tsung, 1969.
Originally published in *T'u-shu-kuan hsüeh-pao* 圖書館學報 (Taipei) 1.1:11-144 (January 1959).

D 41. "T'u shu kuan shu-yü chi" 圖書館術語集. Chin Min-fu 金敏甫, in *T'u-shu-kuan-hsüeh chi-k'an* 圖書館學季刊 (Peking) 4.1:65-94 (March 1930).

D 42. *T'u-shu-kuan-hsüeh chiu-kuo ming-tz'u tui-chao-piao* 圖書館學九國名詞對照表 (Library Terms in Nine Languages). Hsü Neng-yung 徐能庸. Shanghai: Commercial Press, 1930.

PHONETICS AND TRANSCRIPTIONS

Since the Chinese script is nonphonetic it became necessary to develop ways to express the phonetic values of the Chinese characters. A certain Sun Yen 孫炎 of the Wei dynasty (3rd cent. A.D.) is credited by tradition with having evolved the so-called *fan-ch'ieh* 反切 system for this purpose in connection with the transcription of Buddhist terms, (see Kenneth Chen,

Buddhism in China: A Historical Survey. Princeton University Press 1964, p. 479). The *fan-ch'ieh* system is a "cumbersome system of giving pronunciation of characters by two other characters, first giving consonant, second giving vowel formation." (Lin Yutang, *Chinese English Dictionary* [E 60], p. 1168).

Suggested readings on the *fan-ch'ieh* system:

D 43. *ZH Guide: An Introduction to Sinology*. George A. Kennedy. New Haven: Yale University Press 1953, pp. 141-159.

D 44. "Fan-ch'ieh ch'i-yüan lun'反切起源論. Kao Ming高明, in *Wen-chiao lun-ts'ung*文教論叢. Taipei: Cheng-chung, 1971, pp. 153 ff.

D 45. "Lun kuang-yün fan-ch'ieh ken kuo-yü yin-tu"論廣韻反切跟國語音讀. Hsü Shih-ying 許世英, in *Wen-chiao lun-ts'ung* 文教論叢. Taipei: Cheng-chung, 1971, pp. 171 ff.

D 46. "The Chiehyun Problem Re-examined." N. G. D. Malmquist, in *Papers of the Committee on International Cooperation* (*Far Eastern Language Institute*, University of Michigan, Ann Arbor) Vol. 4:10-8 (1973).

D 47. "New Proofs of the Origin of Fan-yü." Li Wei-feng, in *Tamkang Journal* (Taipei) 5:88-112 (November 1966).

D 48. "Some Proleptical Remarks on the Evolution of Archaeic Chinese." Peter Boodberg, in *HJAS* 2.3:354 ff. (1937). Also read: Boodberg's eulogy in *JAOS* 94.1:1-7 (Jan.-March 1974).

The *fan-ch'ieh* system of phonetization is of particular interest to research in Chinese phonology as it is relevant to the reconstruction of ancient Chinese pronunciation.

From the 17th century on, Westerners arriving in China transcribed the sounds of the Chinese language. Each nationality and each observer had his own alphabetization system.

However, due to the preponderance of British influence in the 18th century, the British Wade-Giles system gradually became the most widely used. Sir Thomas Francis Wade (1818-1895) had devised a system for his elementary handbook of Chinese, and Herbert A. Giles (1845-1935) revised and popularized the system in his *Chinese-English Dictionary* [E 56] of 1892.

In 1918, Chinese philologists evolved their own system of phonetic writing, presumably inspired by the Japanese *kana*. This Chinese syllabary is called *chu-yin tzu-mu* 注音字目 or *chu-yin fu-hao* 注音符號, but is popularly referred to as *po-p'o-mo-fo*, from the first four sounds represented in the system. A full table of this transcription system is reproduced on p. 27.

About 10 years later, Chinese linguistics scholars also devised a new system of latinization or romanization, i.e. a Western alphabetic transcription of the sounds of the Chinese language. This is the *gwoyeu romatzh* system. Refer to the phonetic dictionary, *Kuo-yü tzu-tien* 國語字典 [E 53] for an example of this system.

A revised version of this transcription, based partially on Russian drafts, is the system evolved on the mainland, the so-called pinyin 拼音 system, which has recently gained much international acceptance. The pinyin system is used, for instance, in the *Hsin-hua tzu-tien* 新華字典 [E 55].

Suggested readings on romanization:

D 49. *Chinese English Dictionary of Modern Usage.* Lin Yutang. Hongkong: Hongkong Chinese University, 1972, pp. xxvi-xviii.

D 50. *Science and Civilization in China.* Joseph Needham. Cambridge,: Cambridge University Press. Vol. 1 (1954), pp. 8 and 23-7.

D 51. *Introduction aux Etudes d'Histoire Contemporaine, 1898-1949.* Jean Chesnaux and John Lust. Paris: Mouton, pp. 110 ff.

D 52. "Modifying the Romanization of Chinese." Barry

Keenan, in *Asian Studies Professional Review*, (Association for Asian Studies Ann Arbor, Mich.) 5:46-7 (Fall/Spring 1975/76).

D 53. *Guide to Transliterated Chinese in the Modern Peking Dialect.* Ireneus Laszlo Legeza, comp. Leiden: Brill, 1968-1969. 2 vols.

The most comprehensive conversion table of the currently used international and European systems. Also contains a history of transliterations up to the 1958 pinyin.

國音字母表

ㄅ B 伯	ㄆ P 潑	ㄇ M 莫	ㄈ F 佛	ㄪ V [illegible](蘇音)
ㄉ D 德	ㄊ T 特	ㄋ N 訥		ㄌ L 肋
ㄍ G 格	ㄎ K 客	ㄫ NG 額(蘇音)	ㄏ H 赫	
ㄐ J(i) 基	ㄑ CH(i) 欺	ㄬ GN 尼(蘇音)	ㄒ SH(i) 希	
ㄓ J 知	ㄔ CH 痴		ㄕ SH 詩	ㄖ R 日
ㄗ TZ 資	ㄘ TS 雌		ㄙ S 思	(以上聲母)
ㄚ A 啊	ㄛ O 喔	ㄜ E 婀	ㄝ E 厄(蘇音)	
ㄞ AI 哀	ㄟ EI 欸	ㄠ AU 熬	ㄡ OU 歐	
ㄢ AN 安	ㄣ EN 恩	ㄤ ANG 昂	ㄥ ENG 亨	
ㄦ EL 兒				
ㄧ(直行作一) I 衣		ㄨ U 烏	ㄩ IU 迂	(以上韻母)

ㄧㄚ IA 鴉	ㄧㄛ IO 唷	ㄧㄝ IE 耶	ㄧㄞ IAI 崖
ㄧㄠ IAU 腰	ㄧㄡ IOU 幽	ㄧㄢ IAN 烟	ㄧㄣ IN 因
ㄧㄤ IANG 央	ㄧㄥ ING 英		
ㄨㄚ UA 蛙	ㄨㄛ UO 窩	ㄨㄞ UAI 歪	ㄨㄟ UEI 威
ㄨㄢ UAN 灣	ㄨㄣ UEN 溫	ㄨㄤ UANG 汪	ㄨㄥ UENG 翁*
ㄩㄝ IUE 曰	ㄩㄢ IUAN 淵	ㄩㄣ IUN 氳	ㄩㄥ IONG 雍

(以上結合韻母)

*獨用作UENG, 前拼聲母時作ONG, 讀如蘇音之翁

E. Dictionaries.

The student is again reminded that only a small selection of the important dictionaries can be listed in this manual. The list will be divided into ancient and modern dictionaries and a number of the modern subject dictionaries will be listed under the pertinent subject, such as biography, history, religion, etc., if that subject is treated separately.

ANCIENT DICTIONARIES

Suggested reading:

E 1. *Chung-kuo ku-tai ti tzu-tien* 中國古代的字典. Liu Yeh-ch'iu 劉叶秋. Peking: Chung-hua, 1963.
A good introduction to the study of ancient dictionaries.

Ancient Semantic Dictionaries.

The Chinese term for semasiology, the study of the meaning of words, is *hsün ku hsüeh* 訓詁學 Six of the major dictionaries which fall into this category will be discussed in this section.

The *Erh-ya* 爾雅

This is the oldest known Chinese dictionary and perhaps the oldest in the world. Its origin is in doubt. although it is certainly of high antiquity. Since it has always been associated with the interpretation of the venerable texts of classical times, it was elevated to the status of a classic when the *Shih-san-ching* 十三經 edition of the classics was compiled in the *k'ai-ch'eng* 開成 era (836-840) of the T'ang dynasty. Actually, it may appear to us to be less a dictionary than an inventory of words which occurred in writings up to the late Chou times. The words are classified under nineteen abstract and concrete headings, such as, 1. Definitions, 2. Concepts, 3. Explanation of Words, 4. Family Relations, 5. Dwellings, etc.

The following two lines from the *Erh-ya*: illustrate the nature of the contents:

> 賚貢錫畀予貺，賜也 (To bestow is: to donate, present, award, grant, give, confer)
> 春祭曰祠．夏祭言祖 (The spring sacrifice is called *tz'u*, the summer sacrifice is called *yüeh*)

E 2. *Erh-ya* 爾雅. With commentary by Kuo P'u 郭璞 (276-324). Shanghai: Commercial Press, 1929. In series *SPTK*.

E 3. *Erh-ya yin-te* 爾雅引得 ("Index to *Erh-ya*") Peking: Harvard-Yenching Institute, 1942. In series: *Harvard-Yenching Institute Sinological Index Series*, suppl. no 18.
A complete and collated text of the *Erh-ya* precedes the index.

Suggested readings on the *Erh-ya*:

E 4. "The Erh-ya and Other Synonymicons." A. von Rosthorn. Translated from the original German by Ernst Wolff in *Journal of the Chinese Language Teachers Association* 10.3:137-45 (October 1975).

E 5. "The Encyclopedia in China." Wolfgang Bauer, in *Cahiers d'Histoire Mondiale* 9.3:666-7 (October 1975).

The *Hsiao Erh-ya* 小爾雅

Judging by its title, this work may have been meant as a supplement to the *Erh-ya*, but the origin and authorship of the *Hsiao Erh-ya* are also unknown. It is a lexicon believed to have been compiled in early Han times. It is arranged in a similar manner to the *Erh-ya*, but with a different vocabulary and a more limited scope (thirteen chapters compared with *Erh-ya's* nineteen).

Suggested reading:

E 6. *Ssu-k'u t'i-yao* 四庫提要 [G 4], vol. 1, pp. 909-910.

E 7. *Chung-kuo ti ku-tai tzu-tien* [E 1], pp. 88-90.

E 8. "Hsiao Erh-ya k'ao shih" 小爾雅考釋. Hsü Lao-chün 許老君, in *Shih-fan ta-hsüeh kuo-wen yen-chiu-so chi-k'an* 師範大學國文研究所集刊 18:209-320 (1974).

The *Shih-ming* 釋名

This is a glossary compiled by Liu Hsi 劉熙 about 200 A.D. in an arrangement similar to the *Erh-ya*, but with 1,500 items under 27 headings, e.g.: Heaven, Earth, Parts of the Body, etc. Each single word has a short semantic explanation as well as a unique kind of "sound gloss," *yin-hsün* 音訓; for instance:

犂利也利則發土絕草也

(The character 'plow' is to be pronounced *li*; it is sharp ["li"], therefore opens up the soil and cuts weeds)

Although traditionally classed as a *hsün-ku* 訓詁 text, an exegesis to the classics, the work was apparently meant as a pronunciation guide as well as a dictionary. At present, it is highly esteemed as a key to late-Han prounciation. See:

E 9. Linguistic Studies of the Shih-ming: Initials and Consonant Clusters. N. C. Bodman. Cambridge, Mass.: Harvard Univ. Pr., 1954, especially p. 17.

Much additional information on the *Shih-ming* may be found in the substantial reviews of Bodman's book, e.g.:

E 10. Review by L. M. Serruys in *Asia Major* 6.2:137-99 (1958).

E 11. Review by Li Fang-kuei in *Language* 21:153-5 (1955).

E 12. Review by Roy A. Miller in *T'oung Pao* 44:266-87 (1956).

E 13. Review by Tung T'ung-ho in *Far Eastern Quarterly* 14:408 (1955).

The *Kuang-ya* 廣雅

Obviously meant as a continuation and supplement of the *Erh-ya* (廣="enlarging on"), the *Kuang-ya* was compiled by Chang I 張揖, a scholar 博士, who lived in the latter part of the 3rd century. It has long lists of synonyms in nineteen categories. However, being a much later work, it has a wider scope and adduces much more literature as compared with the *Erh-ya*. For a concordance, see:

E 14. *Kuang-ya so-yin* 廣雅索引. ("A Concordance to *Kwang Ya*") Chou Fa-Kao 周法高 editor-in-chief, Hongkong: Chinese University Press, 1977.

The *Fang-yen* 方言

This is the first dictionary of dialects. Its full title makes its origin and purpose even more obvious: 輶車使者絕代語釋別國方言 (Explanations of words of times immemorial and of dialects of other regions as collected by imperial messengers in light carriages). The authorship of this work is disputed but generally ascribed to Yang Hsiung 揚雄 (B.C. 53-18 A.D.). The following representative line may illustrate the kinds of information contained in the *Fang-yen*:

陳楚之間凡人獸乳而雙產謂之釐孳

(In the Ch'en and Ch'u region, twins born to humans or to animals were called *li-tzu*)

Suggested readings for a further study of the *Fang-yen*:

E 15. *The Chinese Dialects of the Han Times According to the Fang-yen*. Paul L. Serruys. Berkeley: University of California Press, 1959.

E 16. *Fang-yen chiao-chien* 方言校箋 ("Index du *Fang-yen*"), Centre d'Etudes Sinologiques de Peking Peking, 1951. In series: Index, Centre Franco-Chinois d'Etudes Sinologiques, no. 14.

In 1942 this series continued the indexing work started by

the Harvard-Yenching Institute in Peking, which was closed down due to the outbreak of the Pacific War. The present volume contains a collated text of the *Fang-yen*.

The *Yü-p'ien* 玉篇

The original compilation of this work is said to have been completed in 543 A.D. and authorship is ascribed to Ku Yeh-wang 顧野王 (519-581) of the Liang 梁 dynasty, but it was probably considerably altered in later recensions. The arrangement of the *Yü-p'ien* follows in many respects the *Shuo-wen chieh-tzu*, an earlier etymological dictionary [E 21]; all characters are classified according to a system of 542 radicals.

Suggested readings on the *Yü-p'ien:*

E 17. "Liang Ku Yeh-wang 'Yü-p'ien'" 梁顧野王玉篇 Liu Yeh-ch'iu, in *Chung-kuo ku-tai ti tzu-tien* [E 1] pp. 23-8.

E 18. "Manuscrits chinois au Japon." Paul Pelliot, in *T'oung Pao* 23:29-30 (1924).

E 19. "Yü P'ien." W. Hummel, in *Report of the Librarian of Congress for 1933*. See [B 15], the relevant article on the *Yü-p'ien* is in vol. 1, pp. 469-70.

Ancient Etymological Dictionaries

The Chinese have understandably always been interested in the historical development of their writing system. Works on etymology—*wen-tzu-hsüeh* 文字學—were classed as part of *hsiao-hsüeh* 小學 (minor scholarship), presumably because they were considered a part of the elementary study of characters. See:

E 20. *Hsiao-hsüeh shu-lüeh* 小學述略. Chang Ping-lin 張炳麟. Published with a *pai-hua* translation in *Ta-hsüeh kuo-wen ts'an-k'ao tzu-liao hui-pien* 大學國文參考資料彙編. Hongkong: Ch'ung-chi hsüeh-yüan, rev. ed. 1970, pp. 54-66.

Popular myth has credited the legendary emperor Fu Hsi 伏羲 and the equally legendary figure of Ts'ang Chieh 倉頡 with the invention of writing. Articles on these figures may be found in:

Chinese Biographical Dictionary [L 9].
Dictionary of Chinese Mythology [M 13].
Mythology of All Races, vol. 8, "Chinese" [M 14].

In the 9th century B.C., a semi-historical figure, Shih Chou 史籀, a scribe of King Hsüan 宣 of the Chou dynasty, is credited with having standardized and cataloged all Chinese characters then extant. His work, the *Shih Chou p'ien* 史籀篇, is still mentioned in Pan Ku's *Han-shu i-wen-chih* but has not come down to our day. A similar book, the *Chi-chiu p'ien* 急就篇, which has come down to us, seems nothing more than a collection of words for elementary instruction.

The first work that truly deserves to be called an etymological dictionary is the *Shuo-wen chieh-tzu* 說文解字 (Explaining single graphs and analyzing composite graphs) compiled by Hsü Shen 許愼, who lived around 100 A.D.

E 21. *Shuo-wen chieh-tzu ku-lin* 說文解字詁林. Ting Fu-pao 丁福保 Shanghia: I-hsüeh shu-chü, preface dated 1930. Taipei repr: I-wen, 1970; Commercial Press, 1966; Ting-wen, 1978.
This is an edition of the *Shuo-wen* that brings together all commentaries as well, and reproduces, as far as they were available at the time of compilation, the oracle and bronze inscription forms of the various characters. See Teng and Biggerstaff, p. 140 on various other editions; also read:

E 22. "Ting Fu-pao." Howard L. Boorman, in *Biographical Dictionary* [L 30] vol. 1, pp. 269-70.
The remarkable biography of Ting Fu-pao.

The *Shuo-wen*, apart from its function as a dictionary, also embodies a theory of the historical development of the Chinese writing system. In the foreword to the *Shuo-wen*, Hsü Shen enumerates six principles, the *liu shu* 六書, that are said to have governed the development of the Chinese characters. We must bear in mind, however, that Hsü Shen was already about 1,000 years removed from the first stylistic reform that put an end to whatever may have remained of earlier archaeic writing forms, and that he was about 2,000 to 3,000 years removed from the birth of the Chinese writing system out of the neolithic picture-writing that no doubt had been its ancestor. While Hsü Shen may have had access to the *Shih Chou p'ien*, he had no knowledge of the Shang-Yin 商殷 script forms that we have at our disposal, thanks to the discovery of the inscribed oracle bones. Hsü's explanations are therefore to be accepted only with reservations; they frequently are nothing but *ad hoc*, speculative stop-gap devices, which may be useful as aids to memorizing characters, but which cannot claim historical or scientific correctness as explanations of the evolution of written forms.

For a translation of Hsü Shen's foreword see:

E 23. "Problems of the Study of the *Shuo-wen chieh-tzu*." Roy Andrew Miller. Unpublished Ph.D. dissertation at Columbia University, 1953.

For a descriptive table of the *liu-shu* and the varying English translations of these six principles, see p. 35. For a detailed study of the six principles, see:

E 24. *The Six Scripts: or The Principles of Chinese Writing.* Tai T'ung 戴侗 (fl. 1275), translated by L. C. Hopkins. Cambridge: Cambridge University Press, 1954.

E 25. "Human Bodily Gestures and the Formation of Chinese Characters." John S. Tong, in *Journal of the Chinese Language Teachers Association* 11.1:39-47 (February 1976).

On the *Shuo-wen* in general, read:

The LIU SHU 六書 according to HSÜ SHEN

	Wade-Giles	Lin Yutang	EW after E. Reifler	Example
象形 *hsiang hsing*	pictorial	pictographs	pictures	山魚馬
指事 *chih shih*	indicative	pictures of action	indicative	上下
會意 *hui i*	suggestive	ideographs	logical compounds	好信
形聲 *hsing sheng* or 諧聲 *hsieh sheng*	phonetic	phonetic symbols	phonetic compounds	錢騎
轉注 *chuan chu*	deflected	figurative extension	mutually explanatory compounds	老考
假借 *chia chieh*	adoptive	making one form stand for another word	phonetic loans	來萬

E 26. *Postface of the Shuo-wen chieh-tzu, the First Comprehensive Chinese Dictionary*. K. L. Thern. Dept. of East Asian Languages and Literature, University of Wisconsin Madison, 1966. (Wisconsin China series, 1).

E 27. *Chinese Characters.* Leon Wieger. Hsien-hsien: Catholic Mission Press, 1914. Repr 2.
The original French edition and the English edition both have seen several editions. However, students should be cautioned against the explanations and deductions found in the etymological lessons in this work. It commits the fallacy, very common in this field of scholarship, of allowing personal imagination to take over when scientific proof is lacking. Also because of its early date of publication Wieger's work does not take into account any of the findings from the oracle bone studies.

The mention of oracle bones shall not pass without reference to the basic works on the discovery and significance of these important finds:

E 28. "The Oracle Bones." H. C. Creel, in *Birth of China*. New York: Raynal and Hitchcock, 1937, pp. 21-6.

This was for a long time considered the standard account of the discovery of the oracle bones, but is now disputed by the following work:

E 29. "Les inscriptions des Shang sur carapaces de tortue et sur os." J. A. Lefeuvre, in *T'oung Pao* 61.1-3:1-82 (1975).

Suggested further readings:

E 30. *Fifty Years of Studies in Oracle Inscriptions.* Tung Tso-pin (1895-1963). Tokyo: Center for East Asian Cultural Studies, 1964.

E 31. *Chia-ku-hsüeh liu-shih nien* 甲骨學六十年. Yen I-p'ing 嚴一平. Taipei: I-wen, 1965.
The author was a student of Tung Tso-pin.

E 32. *Les Jiaguwen: Essay Bibliographique et Synthese des Etudes.* M. Charistian Deydier. Paris: Ecole Francaise d'Extreme-Orient, 1976.
Note the valuable bibliography.

Ancient Phonological Dictionaries

The ancient phonological dictionaries were compiled mainly to serve as rhyming dictionaries. In modern times they are highly appreciated and valued by scholars of linguistics as primary sources on ancient pronunciation. The earliest of these dictionaries are the *Ch'ieh-yün* 切韻, published 601 A.D. by Lu Fa-yen 陸法言 and others, and a later edition, the *T'ang-yün* 唐韻, published 715 A.D. Except for some fragments, both these works are lost. However, a third recension, the *Kuang-yün* 廣韻, published 1007 A.D., based on the material in the *Ch'ieh-yün* and *T'ang-yün*, has come down to us and is now the mainstay of phonological research into ancient Chinese pronunciations.

Suggested readings:

E 33. "Works on Pronunciation," in Teng and Biggerstaff pp. 146-7.
Note in particular the comprehensive listing of *Kuang-yün* editions.

E 34. "China: Historical Linguistics." Nicholas C. Bodman, in *Current Trends in Linguistics* edited by Thomas A. Sebeok. The Hague: Mouton, vol. 2 (1967) 3-58.
Note pp. 8-13 on phonology and the selected bibliography at the end of the article.

E 35. "Bibliography of Chinese Linguistics." William S. Y. Wang, in *Current Trends in Linguistics*, 188-499.
This is a more elaborate bibliography than the preceding one, with several entries on phonology.

E 36. *Kuang-yün sheng-hsi* 廣韻聲系. Shen Chien-shih 沈兼士. Peking: Fu-jen University, 1945. Reprinted in Taiwan.

A recast of the *Kuang-yün* arranged to indicate the principles of phonetic derivation.

E 37. "On the *Kuang-yün sheng-hsi*." Achilles Fang, in *Monumenta Serica* 11:123-9 (1946).
A substantial review of [E 36].

Suggested readings in Chinese on the *Kuang-yün*:

E 38. *Kuang-yün yen-chiu* 廣韻研究. Chang Shih-lu 張世祿. Shanghai: Commercial Press, 1933. Reprinted Taiwan, 1966.

E 39. *Chung-kuo yin-yün-hsüeh* 中國音韻學. Wang Li 王力. Shanghai: Commercial Press, 1936.

E 40. "Ts'ung *Ch'ieh-yün* tao *Kuang-yün*" 從切韻到廣韻 Li Yung-fu 李永富, in *Ta-lu tsa-chih* 大陸雜誌 19.2:9 and 25 and 19.10:3 and 21 (1959).

E 41. *Chi-yün* 集韻. Ting Tu 丁度 and others. Taipei: Shang-wu, 1965. In series *Wan-yu wen-k'u hui-yao* 萬有文庫薈要, No. 442-56.
A later phonological dictionary compiled at the request of Sung scholars to update the *Kuang-yün*. It possibly dates from 1067 and has about 20,000 more entries than the *Kuang-yün*.

E 42. *Chi-yün yen-chiu* 集韻研究. Ch'iu Ch'i-yang 邱棨鐊. Taipei: Cho Shao-lan 卓少蘭, 1974.
A lengthy dissertation (1,234 pages) with an abstract in English.

MODERN DICTIONARIES

A listing of all existing Chinese dictionaries is being attempted by the CETA (Chinese-English Translation Assistance) Group located at Kensington, Maryland. As a preliminary step the group has produced:

E 43. *A Compilation of Chinese Dictionaries*. Sandra Hixson

and J. Mathias. New Haven, Conn.: Far Eastern Publications, Yale University, 1975.
A preliminary listing of over 1000 titles.

Another valuable comprehensive listing is:

E 44. *Chinese-English and English-Chinese Dictionaries in the Library of Congress: An Annotated Bibliography*. Robert Dunn. Washington, D.C.: Library of Congress, 1977.
Note the limitations as to scope and location, but the list contains 569 items with excellent annotations, descriptive and evaluative, and is provided with author, title, and Chinese character indexes. Library of Congress call numbers are given for all items.

Roughly, modern dictionaries may be divided into general language dictionaries and dictionaries of special fields.

General Language Dictionaries

CHINESE TO CHINESE

E 45. *K'ang-hsi tzu-tien* 康熙字典. Completed 1716 under imperial auspices.
The publication of this dictionary inaugurated the modern era of Chinese lexicography. It groups all characters under 214 radicals. Read Teng and Biggerstaff, pp. 129-30. For a recent edition see *Hsin-hsiu k'ang-hsi tzu-tien* 新修康熙字典. Edited by Kao Shu-fan 高樹藩. Taipei: 1979. This is a new typeset recension with pronunciation glosses.

E 46. *Chung-hua ta tzu-tien* 中華大字典. Hsü Yüan-kao 徐元誥 and others. Shanghai: Chung-hua, 1916. Reprinted Taiwan, 1960.
Published just 200 years after the K'ang-hsi dictionary, this is "the best and the most nearly complete dictionary of its kind that has yet been published." (Teng and Biggerstaff, p. 131)

At about the same time the first modern phrase dictionaries appeared:

E 47. *Tz'u-yüan* 辭源. Lu Erh k'uei 陸爾奎 and others. Shanghai: Commercial Press, 1915. Reprinted Taiwan, 1965.
This has had many supplemented and revised editions. See Teng and Biggerstaff, pp. 132-3.

E 48. *Tz'u-hai* 辭海. Shu Hsin-ch'eng 舒新城 and others. Shanghai: Chung-hua, 1936. Reprinted Taiwan, 1948.
Attempts to improve on the preceding dictionary. See Teng and Biggerstaff, pp. 133-4.

Both the *Tz'u-yüan* and the *Tz'u-hai* have been extremely popular, but they are now considered ideologically objectionable and are being subjected to revision on the mainland. See Harold Richter, "Neue Chinesische Woerterbuecher" in *Oriens Extremus* 23:225-43 (December 1976). The first revised edition to come out is:

E 49. *Tz'u-hai (1965 nien hsin-pien pen)* 辭海(1965年新編本). Tz'u-hai pien-chi wei-yüan-hui. Hongkong: Chung-hua, 1979.
Two large volumes of 4,257 pages, in abbreviated characters with pinyin index and other valuable appendices. By size and content so much updated that it bears little resemblance to the 1936 edition. Also published in a three-volume edition.

Note also:

E 50. *ZH Guide, an Introduction to Sinology.* George A. Kennedy (1901-1960). Sinological Seminar, Yale University. New Haven, 1953.
Primarily meant as a guide to the 1936 *Tz'u-hai*, it contains much useful sinological information; see table of contents.

For study of classical Chinese, all of the above phrase dictionaries have been overshadowed by the work of a Japanese sinologue:

E 51. *Dai Kan-Wa jiten* 大漢和辭典. Morohashi Tetsuji 諸橋轍次. Tokyo: Daishūkan, 1957-1960. 12 vols. and 1 index vol.
Although strictly speaking this is a Chinese-Japanese dictionary, the preponderance of Chinese quotations and Chinese characters in the explanations makes it also useful for those without knowledge of or with limited knowledge of Japanese. It is by far the most comprehensive dictionary of words and phrases in classical to premodern Chinese.

E 52. *Chung-wen ta tz'u-tien* 中文大辭典. Chang Ch'i-yün 張其昀 and others. Taipei: Institute of Advanced Chinese Studies, 1962-1968. 38 volumes and 2 index volumes.
Appears to be a Chinese translation of the *Dai Kan-Wa Jiten*. For China scholars it is sometimes more convenient to use, because composite phrases are arranged by stroke count of the second character, while the *Dai Kan-Wa jiten* has them arranged according to Japanese pronunciation.

Among the large number of other Chinese-Chinese dictionaries, the following deserves special mention:

E 53. *Kuo-yü tz'u-tien* 國語辭典 (Kwoyeu Tsyrdean). Shanghai: Commercial Press, 1937. Reprinted Taiwan, 1966.
Read: Teng and Biggerstaff, p. 134. This is the collective work of a group of modern Chinese scholars of linguistics. Characters are arranged in the order of the Chinese phonetic syllabary (bo-po-mo-fo) and pronunciation is given in the national phonetic alphabet as well as in *gwoyeu romatzh*, a forerunner of the *pinyin* system of romanization (see p. 25). The *Kuo-yü tz'u-tien* is highly regarded for its accurate reflection of standard Chinese pronunciation and has come to be recognized by all American East

Asiatic libraries as the final authority in matters of pronunciation.

Suggested reading:

E 54. *A Guide to Gwoyeu Tsyrdean*. Grace Wan. Taipei: Chinese Materials and Research Aids Service Center, 1970.
This 43-page guide is what one might expect as an introduction. It is a description of the dictionary's organization, with short elucidation of phonetic symbols (bo-po-mo-fo), lexical terms, and tone marks (same as used by Lin Yutang [E 60].

E 55. *Hsin-hua tzu-tien* 新華字典 (Xinhua zidian). Peking: Shang-wu, 1971.
A very handy 10x13 cm. pocket dictionary. Characters arranged alphabetically according to the pinyin system. Available with either four-corner or radical indexes.

CHINESE TO ENGLISH

The following are the better known modern Chinese-English dictionaries:

E 56. *A Chinese-English Dictionary*. Herbert A. Giles. London: Kelly & Walsh, 1892; Rev. and enl. ed. 1912. Repr 1.
At the time of it publication this was an invaluable contribution to Chinese studies and for decades, the best available Chinese-English dictionary. It is still useful for the classical and premodern literature. It contains 13,848 characters. Read Robert Dunn [E 44] #410 on pp. 79-80.

E 57. *Mathews' Chinese-English Dictionary*. R. H. Mathews. Shanghai: China Inland Mission Press, 1931. Reprinted by the Harvard University Press in 1943.
Another invaluable tool for pre-1931 Chinese. It contains 7,785 characters and over 104,000 combinations; see Robert Dunn [E 44] #422, p. 82.

E 58. *A Modern Chinese-English Dictionary for Students*. C.

C. Huang. Lawrence, Kansas: University of Kansas Press, 1968.

Intended for the student of modern (including communist) documents and literature. It also lists simplified characters and is arranged in alphabetical order by pinyin, indexed by four basic elements of the first stroke. Its English equivalents are excellent. Unfortunately, it is now out of print.

E 59. *Tsui-hsin shih-yung Han Ying tz'u-tien* 最新實用漢英辭典 ("A New Practical Chinese-English Dictionary"). Liang Shih-ch'iu 梁實秋. Taipei: Far East Book Company, 1972.

It contains 7,331 characters and some 80,000 entries. "One of the most easy to use for all students of Chinese." (Robert Dunn [E 44] #419, pp. 81-2.)

E 60. *Lin Yutang's Chinese-English Dictionary of Modern Usage.* Lin Yutang 林語堂 Hongkong: Chinese University, 1972. It contains about 8,000 characters and about 100,000 entries in a somewhat unconventional arrangement, a kind of "two corner" system, but remarkable for the excellent modern English equivalents for characters and multicharacter compounds, see Robert Dunn [E 44] # 419, pp. 81-2

Suggested readings:

E 61. "The Recent Chinese-English Dictionaries." A Ronald Walton, in *Journal of the Chinese Language Teachers Association* 11.3:204-8 (October 1976).

E 62. Review of *Chinese-English Dictionary of Modern Usage* by Eugene Ching, in *JAS* 34.2:521-4 (February 1975).

Despite the large number of existing Chinese-English dictionaries, there is still demand voiced for new, more complete dictionaries. Read:

E 63. "New Hope for a Chinese-English Dictionary." Elling

O. Eide, in *Journal of the Chinese Language Teachers Association* 10.2:36-47 (May 1975).

E 64. "CETA's Response to Chinese-English Dictionary Needs." Edwin G. Beal, in *Journal of the Chinese Language Teacher Association* 11.1:58-61 (February 1976).

ENGLISH TO CHINESE

In addition to the dictionaries listed by Robert Dunn [E 44] (#464-517 on pp. 91-101), students should be aware of a volume produced through the cooperative effort on the part of a a number of institutions on the mainland:

E 65. *A New English-Chinese Dictionary.* Hongkong: Joint Publishing Company, 1975.
Excellent in its very comprehensive (1,688 pages) coverage of modern English and American usage (including slang). Includes even "words and phrases that reflect the decadent social phenomena of a dying capitalism." It claims to contain more than 80,000 words.

CHINESE TO OTHER WESTERN LANGUAGES

By now every major country has its Chinese dictionaries from or into the national language. Perhaps the only one of general interest is a French dictionary:

E 66. *Dictionnaire Classique de la Langue Chinoise.* F. S. Couvreur. 3rd edition. Hsien-hsien: Catholic Mission Press, 1930. Repr (1st edition of 1911) Taipei: Kuang-ch'i, 1966.
Despite its age it still maintains its usefulness in work with classical texts, from which it quotes and translates abundantly.

DICTIONARIES OF SPECIAL FIELDS

LANGUAGE AND LITERATURE

Linguistics, Grammar, Particles

For a comprehensive bibliography of the entire field, see:

E 67. *Chinese Linguistics: A Selected and Classified Bibliography*. Paul Fu-mien Yang 楊福綿. Hongkong: Chinese University of Hongkong, 1974.
This is a non-annotated bibliography which "focuses on modern and contemporary scientific contributions to Chinese linguistics." Note the wide scope revealed in its table of contents and read the foreword. Includes section on "Dictionaries and Encyclopedias" (pp. 6-8).

Since Chinese lacks the kind of morphology found in Indo-European languages, many grammatical functions are performed by the "particles," called *hsü-tzu* 虛字 in Chinese (all other words are called *shih-tzu* 實字). Chinese grammarians have therefore paid much attention to particles, explaining their meaning and use in dictionary-like works, such as:

E 68. *Chu-tzu pien-lüeh* 助字辨略. Liu Ch'i 劉淇 fl. 1711). Latest editions: Peking: Chung-hua, 1954; Hongkong: Nan-kuo, 1960; Taiwan; Kai-ming, 1960.

E 69. *Ku-shu hsü-tzu chi-shih* 古書虛字集釋. P'ei Hsüeh-hai 裴學海. Shanghai: Commercial Press, 1934.
Reprinted in Peking 1954 and Taiwan: Kuang-wen, 1962.

E 70. *Tz'u ch'üan* 詞詮. Yang Shu-ta 楊樹達. Shanghai: Commercial Press, 1928.
Peking Repr: Chung-hua, 1954; Taiwan: Commercial Press, 1959.

English dictionaries of the particles are:

E 71. *Wenli Particles*. J. J. Brandt. Peking: North China Union

Language School, 1929; Hong Kong Repr: Vetch and Lee, Hongkong, 1973.

A handy short outline (172 pages), with many examples.

E 72. *A Dictionary of the Chinese Particles*. W.A.C.H. Dobson. Toronto: University of Toronto Press, 1974.

Although reviewed rather harshly by Pulleyblank in *HJAS* 35:312-8 (1975), this work is useful for its abundant quotations of classical phrases translated into English, illustrating the use of the various particles. See also R. Dunn [E 44] #459, p. 90.

Etymological Dictionaries/Calligraphy Dictionaries

As noted in the discussion of ancient dictionaries of etymology, the Chinese have always given much attention to the development of their writing system. There are two pursuits, namely carving and calligraphy, which have fostered this interest in the old and ancient character forms. Seals and the art of carving seals, using ancient character forms, have remained popular in China over the centuries. Equally appreciated and the object of much endeavor is the art of calligraphy, in many cases practiced with older and ancient styles of character forms, the main types of which are listed on p. 48. There has been an abundance of dictionaries reflecting interest in these pursuits and the following are merely a few examples:

On seal carving:

E 73. *Wei-ch'ing chia-ku wen yüan* 薇廎甲骨文原. Ma Wei-ch'ing 馬薇廎. Yün-lin Hsien: Hu-wei-chen, 1971.

E 74. *Kanji gogen jiten* 漢字語源辭典 ("Etymological Dictionary of Chinese Characters"). Todo Akiyasu 藤堂明保. Tokyo: Gakutosha, 1965.

E 75. *Chin shih ta tzu-tien* 金石大字典. Wang Jen-shou 汪仁壽. Shanghai: Ch'iu-ku-chai, 1926.

Taiwan Repr: Wu-chou, 1960. 4 vols.

E 76. *Ku Chou hui pien* 古籀彙編. Hsu Wen-ching 徐文鏡.

Taipei: Shang-wu, 1963.

E 77. *Ku chuan-wen ta tzu-tien* 古篆文大字典. Tuan Wei-i 段維毅. Taichung: Hsing-hsüeh, 1967.

E 78. *Chung-wen ch'ang yung san ch'ien tzu hsing i shih* 中文常用三千字形義釋. Chang Hsüan 張瑄. Hongkong: Hongkong University Press, 1968.

On Calligraphy:

Chinese calligraphy is an art form and its bibliography therefore belongs to the chapter on "Art" (see, e.g. "Calligraphy" in T. L. Yüan's art bibliography [N 2] p. 2). Here I merely wish to mention etymology-related dictionaries that are meant to serve the calligrapher. Such dictionaries are quite popular also in Japan, and are usually designated as *shu-fa* 書法 dictionaries. They usually display the various historical styles of writing (see table on page 48) side by side, in a *ssu-t'i* 四體, *liu-t'i* 六體 or similar arrangement. Some prefer the white on black reproduction of characters, as of rubbings, with indications of the source from which the "rubbing" had been taken. Examples:

E 79. *Li-tai shu-fa tzu-hui* 歷代書法字彙. Taipei: Ta-t'ung shu-chü, 1972. 1616 pages, 27 cm.

E 80. *Cheng ts'ao li chuan ssu-t'i tzu-tien* 正草隸篆四體字典. Hongkong: Chung-kuo wen-hsüeh wen-tzu yen-chiu-hui, n.d.

Literature in General

E 81. *Dictionary of Oriental Literatures*. Vol. 1: "East Asia." Jaroslav Prusek, general ed., Zbigniew Slupski, ed. of vol. 1. London: Allen and Unwin, 1974.
"The preface describes the work as a brief but reliable and easy reference . . . for the educated but non-specialist reader." Has useful bibliographies appended to its very short articles.

E 82. *A Guide to Eastern Literatures*. David Marshall Lang, ed.

The Different Styles of Chinese Script

1.	甲骨文	*chia ku wen*	oracle bone and shell inscriptions, ca, B.C. 1500.
2.	大 篆	*ta chuan*	great seal script by Shih Chou, therefore also called *ku Chou wen*, ca B.C. 900.
3.	小 篆	*hsiao chuan*	small seal script by Li Ssu, prime minister of Ch'in-shih-huang-ti.*
4.	隸 書	*li shu*	the *li*-style script, or clerical script, of the Han dynasty.
5.	楷 書	*k'ai shu*	the "regular" style (as opposed to 6 and 7 below).
6.	行 書	*hsing shu*	the running style**
7.	草 書	*ts'ao shu*	the "grass script"**

* Cf. *Guide to the Chinese Decorative Script*. Compiled by Eric Grinstead, drawn by Yoshihiko Iizuka. Lund, 1970.

**Cf. *Introduction of Chinese Cursive Script*. By Wang Fang-yü. New Haven, Conn., 1958.

New York: Praeger, 1971.
Chapter entitled "Chinese Literature" by Yin C. Liu and Tao Tao Sanders contains short biographical sketches of about fifty Chinese literary figures, followed by seven pages of bibliography.

Literary Genres

In the course of its centuries of development, Chinese literature has developed various genres, usually associated with a specific period during which the genre evolved or flourished, as, for instance, the *fu* 賦 in the Han dynasty, the *lü-shih* 律詩 in the T'ang dynasty, the *tz'u* 詞 in the Sung dynasty and the *ch'ü* 曲 in the Yüan dynasty. Each genre has its own peculiar prosody and terminology.

For background reading see:

E 83. *Topics in Chinese Literature: Outlines and Bibliographies.* James Robert Hightower. Cambridge, Mass.: Harvard University Press, 1962.

E 84. *The Art of Chinese Poetry.* James J. Y. Liu. Chicago: University of Chicago Press, 1962.

E 85. *Guide to Chinese Poetry and Drama.* Roger R. Bailey. Boston: G. K. Hall, 1973.

E 86. *Guide to Chinese Prose.* Jordan D. Paper. Boston: G. K. Hall, 1973.

E 87. *Chinese Fiction: A Bibliography of Books and Articles in Chinese and English.* Li Tien-yi. New Haven: Yale University, 1968.

E 88. "Publications nouvelles interessant l'histoire de la litterature chinoise." See André Levy in BEFEO 53:279-91 (1966/67).

For Chinese dictionaries that elucidate certain aspects of the prosody, terminology, or diction of Chinese literary genres see:

E 89. *Shih tz'u ch'ü yü tz'u-tien* 詩詞曲語辭典. Chang Hsiang 張相 (1877-1945). Taipei: I-wen, 1957.

E 90. *Tz'u-p'ai hui-shih* 詞牌彙釋. Wen Ju-hsien 聞汝賢, Taipei, [n.p.] 1963.

E 91. *Hsiao-shuo tz'u-yü hui-shih* 小說詞語滙釋. Lu Tan-an 陸澹安. Peking: Ching-hua, 1964. Taiwan repr: Chung-hua, 1968.

E 92. *Chin Yüan hsi-ch'ü fang-yen k'ao* 金元戲曲方言考. Hsü Chia-jui 徐嘉瑞. Rev. ed. Shanghai: Commercial Press, 1957. Reprinted on Taiwan.

Proverbs 俗語 *and Common Sayings* 成語, 諺語

Chinese spoken and written language has always been enriched with an abundance of these phrases. For comprehensive lists of older works on these genres, see Cordier [C 1] columns 3948-3949, and Yüan *China in Western Literature* [C 2]; pp. 460-1. A good Chinese bibliography on this subject is:

E 93. "Chung-kuo yen-yü shu-mu t'i-yao" 中國諺語書目提要 Chu Chieh-fan 朱介凡, in *T'u-shu-kuan hsüeh-pao* 6:84-123 (July 1964).

Chinese proverbs and common sayings have attracted the interest of many lovers of Chinese folklore. The following are some of the better known collections in chronological order:

E 94. *A Manual of Chinese Metaphor*. C. A. S. Williams. Shanghai: Commercial Press, 1920. Reprinted by AMS Press, New York, 1974.

E 95. *Proverbs and Common Sayings from the Chinese*. A. H. Smith. Shanghai: Presbyterian Mission Press, 1902. Repr 1.

E 96. *Dictionary of Chinese Idiomatic Phrases*. Huang Yen-k'ai. Hongkong: Eton Press, 1964.
The most important and voluminous work (1,291 pages)

of this kind. Four-character phrases are given one basic and one idiomatic English rendering, in addition to an explanation of origin. Reviewed critically by Russell Maeth in *JAS* 25:752-4 (1966).

E 97. *Selected Chinese Sayings*. Lai T'ien-ch'ang. 3rd ed. Hongkong: University of Hongkong, 1966.

E 98. *Chinese-English 2000 Selected Chinese Common Sayings*. C. K. Wu 吳志鋼 and K. S. Wu 吳黃燊琇. Hongkong: Chinese Language Research Association, 1968. See Richard Dunn [E 44] #105, p. 20.

E 99. *Chinese Proverbs*. Chiang Ker Chiu 蔣克秋 Singapore, 196-? 2 volumes.

There are a large number of Chinese-Chinese dictionaries of proverbs and common sayings (*ch'eng-yü shou-ts'e* 成語手冊 and *ch'eng-yü tz'u-tien* 成語辭典) of which the following two may serve as examples:

E 100. *Fen-lei ch'eng-yü shou-ts'e* 分類成語手冊. K'o Huai-ch'ing 柯槐青. Shanghai: Hsin-lu, 1947. 2 volumes. Taiwan repr: Pa-t'i, 1953.

E 101. *Chung-kuo ch'eng-yü ta tz'u-tien* 中國成語大辭典. Kao Mo-yeh 高莫野, Hongkong: Shang-hai yin-shu-kuan, 1973.

Couplets 對聯

For centuries the writing of couplets has had an important social function in traditional China. Condolences, congratulatory messages, and New Year door decorations were often written in couplets—a practical application of the highly esteemed calligraphic art. The tradition seems to be continued on Taiwan and it also flourishes on the mainland, where the contents of such couplets have a strongly political flavor. There has never been a shortage of couplet dictionaries, the following are three recent examples:

E 102. *Lung-yen lien-hua* 龍眼聯話. Liu Lung-min 劉隆民. Taipei: Hsüeh-sheng, 1965. 2 volumes.
Contains a short historical outline of Chinese couplet writing in the foreword.

E 103. *Hsin-pien shih-yung tui-lien ch'üan chi* 新編實用對聯全集. Ch'en Chou-hsiung 陳洲雄. Tainan: Fu-han, 1972.

E 104. *Tui-lien* 對聯 *Chinese Couplets, Translated and Annotated.* Lai T'ien-ch'ang, ed. and tr. Hongkong: University of Hongkong, 1969.

Puns 俏皮話, 歇後語

The Chinese *ch'iao-p'i-hua* or *hsieh-hou-yü* is a mixture of proverb, witticism and joke and not merely a play on words as the Western pun. It is a saying in two parts, the first part giving the listener the clue as to what the second part should be. The second part is left unsaid, assuming that the listener knows it or can puzzle it out. Examples:

(a) 貓哭老鼠 mao k'u lao-shu = 假慈悲 chia tz'u-pei
The cat sheds tears for the mouse = false commiseration, hypocrisy.

(b) 外甥打燈籠 wai-sheng ta leng-lung =
照舅 (照舊) Chao chiu (chao chiu)
The nephew carries a lantern = he lights the way for his uncle. (homophonous with: unchanged, as usual)

A collection of such *hsieh-hou-yü* may be found in K'o Huai-ch'ing's *Ch'eng-yü shou-ts'e* [E 100]. A Chinese-English collection is:

E 105. *A Dictionary of Peiping Slanguage* 北平諧後語辭典. Ch'en Tzu-shih 陳子實. Taipei: Ta Chung-kuo, 1969.

Suggested readings:

E 106. "A Tentative Classification and description of the Structure of Peking Common Sayings *(hsieh-hou-yü).*"

L. Kroll, in *JAOS* 86:267-76 (July/September 1966).

E 107. "Pekinger Hsieh-hou-yü." Erich Schmitt, in *Archiv für Ostasien* 1:13-9 (1948). In German.

Dictionaries of New Terms and Phrases

The term "new" is particularly conspicuous in Chinese modern history in connection with two periods. First, the expression *hsin-hsüeh* 新學 (new learning) designates the efforts to absorb Western science and technology with the opening-up of China that followed the Opium War (see the chapter on *hsin-hsüeh* in the Kyoto Research Institute for Humanistic Studies catalog [D 30]. Most of the terms of that era, like telephone, steamship, railway, have already been included in the early modern dictionaries, such as the *Tz'u-hai* and *Tz'u-yüan*.

The second period to which the adjective "new" is frequently attadred is that of the communist take-over of 1949. Here "new terms" means Marxist-Leninist-Maoist terms. A number of dictionaries were published at that time explaining the new terms, which had been unknown to most Chinese before the "liberation" of 1949. Such dictionaries are, for instance.

E 108. *Hsin ming-tz'u shou ts'e* 新名詞手冊. Ts'ang Nien 倉年 , ed. Shanghai, 1949.

E 109. *Hsin chih-shih tz'u-tien* 新知識辭典. Li Chin 李進 and others. Shanghai: Pei-hsin, 1950.

E 110. *Hsin ming-tz'u tz'u-tien* 新名詞辭典. Shanghai: Ch'un-ming, 1949.

As the People's Republic has passed its third decade, the "new terms" are no longer new. Continuous linguistic changes on the mainland, particularly the coining of new slogans, have produced the need for dictionaries of Chinese communist terminology to keep up with the unceasing stream of newly coined words and phrases. The most outstanding examples of such dictionaries are the following:

E 111. *A Chinese-English Dictionary of Communist Terminology*. J. Dennis Doolin and C. P. Ridley. Stanford. California: Hoover Institution Press, 1973.
Despite some shortcomings (see the review by James J. Wrenn in *JAS* 39.3:468-9 (May 1974), this dictionary offers many English equivalents used by mainland Chinese government agencies in their translations.

E 112. *Chinese-English Dictionary of Contemporary Usage*. Chi Wen-shun, with the assistance of John S. Service, Chi-ping Chen and Mei Hsia T. Huang. Berkeley: University of California Press, 1977.
A long-term effort by the Center for Chinese Studies at Berkeley. This dictionary, with over 20,000 terms, is a valuable tool in this area. English equivalents are precise and idiomatic. For some complaints of a formal nature, see the review by Jerry Norman in *JAS* 37.4:752-3 (August 1978).

E 113. *A Comprehensive Glossary of Chinese Communist Terminology* 中共名詞術語辭典. Warren Kuo, editor-in-chief. Taipei: National Chengchi University, 1978.
This is an encyclopedic glossary of compound phrases used in Chinese communist publications and documents. Includes several indexes to help identify phrases. Excellent English equivalents are provided.

E 114. *Glossary of Chinese Political Phrases*. Lau Yee-fui and others. Hongkong: Union Research Institute, 1977.
A glossary similar to the preceding one, also briefly reviewed by Jerry Norman, *JAS* 37.4:752-3 (August 1978).

To which should now also be added a recent mainland publication:

E 114A. *A Chinese-English Dictionary*. By a special group of compilers in the Peking Foreign Languages Institute 北京外國語學院英語系漢英詞典編寫組. Peking, Commercial Press, 1978. 976p.

A cooperative effort of eight years, most helpful in translation work due to the authoritative English equivalents of communist common phrases and slogans. Arrangement is alphabetic by pinyin with an index by radicals.

Readers of German should also consult:

E 115. *Chinesisch-Deutscher Wortschatz; Politik und Wirtschaft der VR China*. Helmut Martin and Tienchi Martin-Liao. Berlin: Langenscheidt, 1977.

Dialect Dictionaries

There are considerable disparities among Chinese dialects, read Chao Yuenren's "Chinese Language–Dialects," in *Encyclopedia Britannica,* 1964 edition). Many dictionaries of individual dialects are available, of which the following may serve as examples:

For Cantonese:

E 116. *The Cantonese Speaker's Dictionary*. Roy T. Cowles. Hongkong: Hongkong University Press, 1965.

E 117. *Cantonese Dictionary: Cantonese-English, English-Cantonese*. Parker Po-fei Huang 黃伯飛. New Haven: Yale University Press, 1970.
"For the student of Cantonese this book is a milestone;" see the review by Fang-yu Wang in *JAS* 30.4:892-3 (August 1971).

For Amoy (Min-nan):

E 118. *Chinese-English Dictionary of Amoy*. Carstairs Douglas. London: Trübner, 1873. Reprint: Taipei: Ku-t'ing, 1970.

E 119. *Amoy-English Dictionary*. Maryknoll Fathers. Taichung, Foreword 1976.

For Hakka:

E 120. *English-Hakka Dictionary*. Taichung: Kuang-ch'i, 1959.

SCIENCE AND TECHNOLOGY DICTIONARIES

There is an abundance of specialized dictionaries, mostly English-Chinese, in every field of science and technology. The most important producers of these dictionaries are:

On Taiwan: The National Institute for Compilation and Translation, 國立編譯館, which is the successor to an institute set up by the Chinese government in 1932, see *Kuo-li pien-i-kuan kai-k'uang* 國立編譯館概況. Taipei, 1961, pp. 4-6.

On the Mainland: K'o-hsüeh ch'u-pan she 科學出版社. Peking. Particularly active since 1974, they have produced dictionaries for instance, on gas turbine installation, electronic circuits, meteorology, macromolecule chemistry, etc.

In the USA: The National Technical Information Service, Department of Commerce. They have recently produced Chinese-English dictionaries on nuclear physics, aviation and space, electronics and computers, etc.

For science and technology terms see also:

E 121. *Modern Chinese-English Technical and General Dictionary*. New York: McGraw-Hill, 1963. 3 vols.
This is a computer-compiled dictionary indexed by pinyin romanization, by characters, and by Chinese telegraph code numbers.

E 122. *Scientific and Technical Chinese: A Textbook of 21 Lessons*. Kao Kung-yi, Thomas Fingar, Carl Crook, and Ernest Chin. Stanford, California: U.S.-China Relations Program, 1978. 2 vols.
Vol. 2 is an English-Chinese glossary with a limited (108 p.) but useful selection of basic terms.

F. Encyclopedias

The traditional Chinese term for encyclopedias is *lei-shu* 類書; in modern times they are called *pai-k'o ch'üan-shu* 百科全書.

Recommended readings:

Teng and Biggerstaff, pp. 83-4.

F 1. "The Encyclopedia in China." Wolfgang Bauer, in *Cahiers d'Histoire Mondiale* 9.3:665-91 (1966).

F 2. *Lei-shu: Old Chinese Reference Works.* Austin Shu. Taipei: Chinese Materials and Research Aids, 1973.

F 3. "Lei-shu". Samuel Couling, in *Encyclopaedia Sinica* [C 14], pp. 296-7.

F 4. "The Luy Shoo 'Cyclopaedias'". A. Wylie, in *Notes* [C 13], pp. 181-9.

F 5. "Bibliography of the Chinese Imperial Collections of Literature." W. I. Meyers, in *China Review* 6.4:1-113; 185-299 (1878).

F 6. *Lei-shu liu-pieh* 類書流別. Chang Ti-hua 張滌華. Shanghai: Commercial Press, 1958.

F 7. *Wen-shih sui-pi* 文史隨筆. Hsü I-shou 徐益壽. Hong Kong: Da Kuang, 1966.

A discussion of the *lei-shu* may be subdivided chronologically.

PRE-T'ANG AND T'ANG ENCYCLOPEDIAS

Encyclopedias have been compiled in China as elsewhere to combine in one book, or set of books, all contemporary human knowledge available. In China encyclopedias began to be compiled as soon as a certain quantity of documented knowledge had been accumulated in the imperial libraries. The first Chinese encyclopedia, called *Huang-lan* 皇覽 (For Imperial Perusal), is said to have been prepared for Emperor Wu Ti of the Wei dynasty (i.e. Ts'ao Ts'ao, 155-220 A.D.) for the purpose of presenting a survey of all knowledge. This work is mentioned in the *Annals of the Sui Dynasty* (隋書卷34經籍志); see also Ho To-yüan [D 6], p. 103. Only fragments of the *Huang-lan* are extant (see e.g., reproduction in the *TSCC* series, no. 172). Later, Chang Hua 張華 (232-300 A.D.) is credited with the compilation of a kind of encyclopedic handbook, the *Po-wu-chih* 博物志 (A Record of All in Nature). The book presently bearing this title–reprinted in the SPPY and TSCC collectaneas–is of doubtful authenticity, but interesting. It is a hodgepodge of legends, folktales, superstitions, etc., without index or systematic arrangement. The *Ssu-k'u t'i-yao* [G 4] therefore does not list it as a *lei-shu*, but rather under the *hsiao-shuo-chia* 小說家 (essayists).

Somewhat similar in nature is the *Chin-lou-tzu* 金樓子 by Liang Yüan-ti 梁元帝 (508-554). The information in this work is grouped under 13 headings, such as "Flourishing Kings" 興王, "Admonitions" 箴戒 "Imperial Consorts" 后妃, "Mourning" 終制, "Precepts (left posthumously) to Sons" 戒子, "Book Collections" 聚書, etc. Again the *Ssu-k'u t'i-yao* does not recognize this work as a *lei-shu*, but lists it under the *tsa-chia* 雜家 (miscellaneous writers). The original text has survived only as included in the *Yung-lo ta-tien* [F 28] and has been copied from there for separate publication.

By the time of the Sui dynasty (589-617), when writing had become highly sophisticated, encyclopedias also functioned as writer's aids, particularly to provide quotations, allusions and other flowery adornments, culled not only from the classics but also from writings of more recent periods. The *Pien-chu* 編珠 is usually mentioned as the first evidence of this trend, although authenticity and dating of this work is disputed, as e.g., by the *Ssu-k'u t'i-yao* compilers. The book catalog of the Chin dynasty (*Chin-shu ching-chi chih* 晉書經籍志) lists several *lei-shu* type book-titles, unfortunately most of them have been lost, such as the *Hsiu-wen-tien yü-lan* 修文殿御覽 and the *Hua-lin pien-lüeh* 華林遍略 which is said to have consisted of 600 *chüan*.

An interesting work that has come down to our times is the *Meng-ch'iu chi-chu* 蒙求集注 (Annotated collection of pupils' pursuits). Though perhaps originally intended as a primer of style, it is listed as a *lei-shu* in the *Ssu-k'u t'i-yao*. Its author is given as Li Han 李瀚 (fl. 746-766) of the later Chin period 後晉. The book consists of a collection of 4-character lines each a pithy mnemonic literary allusion. A short commentary explains the meaning of each; for example:

> 枚乘蒲輪 *Mei Sheng p'u lun* (Mei Sheng and the 'soft' carriage) Commentary: At the time of the former Han, Mei Sheng was official of Ling P'i of Wu. The king harbored traitorous intentions (against the emperor). Mei Sheng counselled against such, but the king did not listen and met his doom. This affair made Mei Sheng famous. When Wu Wang became emperor, Mei Sheng was already quite advanced in age. The emperor sent a "soft" carriage, with wheels wrapped in rushes, to bring him to the Court. Mei Sheng died on the journey.

Similarly, we find the story of poet Chia I and the owl compressed into the phrase *Chia I chi fu* 賈誼忌鵩 (Chia I resents the owl), and the story of Chiang Yen's dream of Kuo P'o 郭濮, who comes to reclaim a pen which embodied his poetic genius, compressed into the phrase *Chiang Yen meng pi* 江淹夢筆 (Chiang Yen's dream of the pen).

The first two works which constitute encyclopedias in the real sense of the word are of a somewhat later period: the *Pei-t'ang shu-ch'ao* 北堂書鈔 and the *I-wen lei-chü* 藝文類聚. While the former is the private work of a single author, therefore more limited in scope, the latter, extending to 100 *chüan*, is a more comprehensive work compiled by an imperial commission. However, in appearance and general layout, both seem to follow a pattern set by earlier works of which we have no knowledge.

F 8. *Pei-t'ang shu-ch'ao* 北堂書鈔. Yü Shih-nan 虞世南 (558-638). Taipei: Wen-hai, 1962. 2 vols.

The author, whose biography appears in both *T'ang-shu*, the official dynastic histories of the T'ang dynasty, probably compiled his encyclopedia when he was in charge of the Sui dynasty archives. The term *pei-t'ang* in the title refers to the section of the palace where the archives were housed. At the height of his career he was appointed member of the Academy of Literature, the *Hung-wen kuan* 宏文館 by Emperor T'ai-tsung of the T'ang, his works are therefore generally attributed to the T'ang era. The *Ssu-k'u t'i-yao* question the authenticity of the presently extant version, which is a Ming edition, repeating the accusation against Ming publishers that they "added and deleted, making arbitrary and presumptious alterations. Their crudeness, foolhardiness and stupidity was justly ridiculed by Ch'ien (Ch'ien Ts'eng 錢曾) and Chu (Chu I-tsun 朱彝尊)."

In its present form the *Pei-t'ang shu-ch'ao* clearly reveals its purpose as a writer's handbook. Quotations from the literature that must have been available at the Sui Court were arranged under 19 main headings, such as (1) Emperors and Kings, (2) Imperial Consorts, (3) Art of Government, (4) Penal Laws, (5) Enfeoffments, etc., down to items of daily life, nature, fauna and flora, variously subdivided.

To give a few examples: under main heading HEAVEN, subheading *Moon*, we find the following quotations and explanations:

夜光謂之月 ("Night brightness" is a reference to the moon). The Po-ya 博雅 (actually *Kuang-ya*, but character 廣 was taboo under Emperor Yang Ti of the Sui dynasty being his personal name) says: " 'Night brightness' is a reference to the moon."

宵曜名夜光 ("Light in the Dark" is a name for "Night Brightness.") Huang-fu Mi 皇甫謐 (215-181) in his *Nien-li* 年歷 (full title: 帝王世紀年歷) says: "As the moon lights up the night, it is named 'night brightness'."

There are 76 such quotations in this chapter on the moon quoting from a large array of writers. An index to the sources in the work is:

F 9. *Pei-t'ang shu-ch'ao yin-shu so-yin* 北堂書鈔引書索引. Yamada Hideo 山田英雄 Taipei: Wen-hai, 1975.

In some instances the quotations are merely excerpts from poems, e.g.:

皎皎照我床 from Ts'ao P'i's poem:
明月皎皎照我床
星漢西流夜未央
(The moon's white light shines on my bed; the Milky Way flows west; the night is not yet spent.)

靈娥上奔月 from Kuo P'o's poem:
翩翩尋靈娥
眇然上奔月
(Flying in search of Fairy Ch'ang O; far, far, rushing to the moon.)

It is particularly these contractions of longer phrases into concise terms that later writers prefer to use in the formal *p'ien-t'i* 駢體 style composition, also in lyrical poetry, especially in the *chüeh-chü* the 4-line poems where space is scarce.

F 10. *I-wen lei-chü* 藝文類聚. Ou-yang Hsün 歐陽詢 (557-648). Peking: Chung-hua, 1965. 2 vols. Taiwan repr: Hsin-hsing, 1969.
The *I-wen lei-chü* (Classical and modern literature assembled by categories) was compiled by an imperial commission headed by Ou-yang Hsün, who first served the Sui, later the T'ang, advancing to membership in the Academy of Literature. His life story is recorded in the both *T'ang-shu*.

In a (readable) introduction to the work, Ou-yang Hsün describes it as follows:

Among the collections of the preceding generation in which their ideas have found expression, the *Wen-hsüan* merely selected literary items and the *Huang-lan* type of survey works only listed facts. Although they brought together a great variety of writings, things could not easily be located in one place. Now, on Imperial Command, we have compiled factual matter together with literary matter, discarding the superficial and eliminating the superfluous, and arranged the treasures of the past according to categories, calling the work *Classified Collection of Classical and Modern Literature*, in a total of 100 *chüan*. Whatever was quoted from literature has not been broken up to be included in the factual accounts. Therefore, the factual notes precede and literature follows, which the reader will find beneficial and the works of the various authors are put to good use. This will facilitate coordination of the modern and the old and will allow us to model ourselves after the ancient classics.

The arrangement is by 43 main categories and altogether almost 700 subdivisions, set in a certain logical sequence, starting with "Heaven," "Four Seasons," "Annual Occurrences," "Earth," "Geographical Divisions," "Mountains," "Waterways," "Propitious Omens," "Emperors and Kings," etc., ending with flora and fauna.

Checking again the section on the Moon, we notice, first of all, a much wider coverage as compared with the *Pei-t'ang shu-ch'ao*. The chapter on the Moon is in three parts. The first part gives 'facts,' i.e. a definition and pertinent descriptive terms; the second part quotes poetry, and the third part poetic prose, *fu* 賦, on the moon.

The descriptive part starts out with a quotation from the old glossary, the *Shih-ming* 釋名 [E 9]:

月闕也滿則缺也晦灰也月死爲灰月光盡似之也
朔蘇也月死復蘇生也弦月半之名也

The Moon is what wanes; once full, it wanes. On the last day of the lunar month it is like ashes. The Moon dies and becomes ashes; it seems as if the Moon's brightness is exhausted. On the first day of the lunar month the Moon revives. The Moon dies and comes to life again. 'Hsien' is a term for the half-moon. . . . (Our literal translation cannot reproduce the homophonic word play of the *Shih-ming*).

The second section consists of almost six pages of the best known 'Moon poems,' quoted in full, and the third section consists of four *fu* on the Moon, of which one, by Hsieh Ling-yün, to my knowledge is nowhere else to be found in contemporary collections:

臥洞房兮當何悅	What happiness in nuptual chambers,
滅華燭兮弄曉月	The wedding candles extinguished, enjoying the Moon at day-break.
昨三五兮既滿	Yesterday, on the 15th, the Moon was full,
浮雲褰兮收泛灔	Today, on the 16th, the Moon begins to wane.
浮雲褰兮收泛灔	Floating clouds recede, an overflowing
明舒照兮殊皎潔	Brightness, soothing light, exquisitely pure and pale.
墀除兮鏡鑑	The steps to the house like shining mirrors,
房櫳兮澄徹	The building itself a translucent white.

(As far as Hsieh Ling-yün's poetry is translatable!)

This indicates the value of the old Chinese encyclopedias as repositories of literature, which, in many cases, has otherwise been lost. For this particular reason, a few further *Lei-shu* of this ancient period may be mentioned herebelow:

F 11. *Po-shih liu-t'ieh* 白氏六帖. Po Chü-i 白居易 (772-846) ascribed author. Taipei: Hsin-hsing, 1969. 2 vols.
See Teng and Biggerstaff, p. 86. A literary encyclopedia in 30 chapters. The term *liu-t'ieh* (six papers) in the title is usually explained as having to do with the examination system of the time, the purpose of the book being to assist candidates for the government examinations. The *Ssu-k'u t'i-yao* [G 4] does not list the original work, but a later edition enlarged to 100 *chüan* compiled by K'ung ch'uan 孔傳 of the Sung dynasty, published under the title:

F 12. *Po K'ung liu-t'ieh* 白孔六帖. K'ung Ch'uan and others. Taipei: Hsin-hsing, 1969. 2 vols.

See Teng and Biggerstaff, p. 87. Also:

F 13. *Le Traité des Examens.* Robert Des Rotours. Paris: Leroux, 1932. Repr 1.

Check and compare the treatment of the Moon in *Po-shih liu-t'ieh*, chapter I, item 4, and the same subject in previously mentioned encyclopedias.

F 14. *Lung-chin feng-sui p'an* 龍筋鳳髓判. Chang Cho 張鷟. Shanghai: Commercial Press, 1937. (In series TSCC #785-786).

This work is a collection of legal and administrative decisions for candidates at administrative examinations to emulate. Each chapter has as heading a brief resume of a criminal or administrative problem, e.g., bribery, divulging state secrets, request by the Turfan ambassador for permission to buy brocade, bows, and arrows, etc., followed by essays giving an appropriate opinion in the ornate style of the period.

F 15. *Ch'u-hsüeh chi* 初學記. Hsü Chien 徐堅. Peking: Chung-hua, 1962. Taiwan repr: Hsin-hsing, 1971.

Read the introduction to the Peking 1962 edition, also the earlier preface dated 1134 which explains that the book was intended by Emperor Hsüan Tsung (713-755) as a textbook, or reference book, for students at the School of Princes. Also check its treatment of the Moon in chapter 1, subdivision 3.

For further study, see:

F 16. *Ta T'ang hsin-yü* 大唐新語. Liu Su 劉肅. Shanghai: Commercial Press, 1937. (In series TSCC #2741-2742).

SUNG ENCYCLOPEDIAS

The large compendia compiled early in the Sung era are often referred to as the *Sung ssu ta shu* 宋四大書 (Four Great Books of the Sung), see:

F 17. *Sung ssu-ta-shu k'ao* 宋四大書考. Kuo Po-kung 郭伯恭. Shanghai: Commercial Press, 1940; Taipei Repr: Commercial Press, 1967.

The "Four Great Books" are: (1) *T'ai-p'ing yü-lan*, (2) *T'ai-p'ing kuang-chi*, (3) *Wen-yüan ying-hua*, and (4) *Ts'e-fu yüan kuei;* they are described in more detail below:

F 18. *T'ai-p'ing yü-lan* 太平御覽. Peking: Chung-hua shu-chü, 1960. Taiwan repr: Commercial Press, 1968.
A group of top-ranking scholars was put to work on this encyclopedia, some suspect in order to detract their attention from meddling in politics. They produced a work of 1,000 *chüan* with 55 main headings (presumably following the *I-ching* 易經繫辭上傳第九章: 凡天地之數五十有五) and 4,558 categories; see Teng and Biggerstaff, p. 88.

Other suggested readings:

F 19. "The Significance of Confusion; the Origin of the T'ai-p'ing yü-lan." J. W. Haeger, in *JAOS* 88.3:401-9 (September 1968).

F 20. *T'ai-p'ing kuang-chi* 太平廣記. Peking: Chung-hua, 1961. Taiwan repr: Hsin-hsing, 1969; Hua-cheng, 1972; Hsi-nan, 1974.
Read Teng and Biggerstaff, p. 125. Despite similarity of name and origin, the TPKC is completely different in content from the TPYL. It is said to have been the repository of all "non-serious" material, that was considered unfit for inclusion into the TPYL. The TPKC contains a large collection of short stories, the nature of which is evident from the first few headings of its 92 main categories:

1.	神仙	Spirits	4.	方士	Necromancers
2.	女仙	Fairies	5.	異人	Strange Men
3.	道術	Magic Arts	6.	異僧	Strange Monks

Even stories under such prosaic headings as "rain," "mountains," "stones," etc. tell of extraordinary events and manifestations of supernatural and occult influences. The TPKC has been a favored source for translators; see:

F 21. *List of Published Translations from Chinese into English, French and German*. Martha Davidson. Ann Arbor, Mich.: Edwards, 1952, p. 88.

However, the work has never been translated in full. For indexes see:

F 22. *T'ai-p'ing kuang-chi p'ien-mu chi yin-shu yin-te* 太平廣記篇目及引書引得 ("Index to T'ai P'ing Kuang Chi"), Teng Ssu-yü 鄧嗣. Taipei: Chinese Materials Research Aid Service Center, 1966. (Reprint of No. 15 of the Harvard-Yenching Sinological Index Series).

F 23. *T'ai-p'ing kuang-chi jen-ming shu-ming so-yin* 太平廣記人名書名索引 Chou Tz'u-chi 周次吉. Taipei: I-wen, 1973.

F 24. *Wen-yüan ying-hua* 文苑英華. Taipei: Hua-wen, 1965. 12 vols. and index (1967).
Read Wylie's *Notes* [C 13], p. 240; also Librarian of Congress Annual Report [B 15], vol. 1, p. 78.
This is a collection of "polite literature subsequent to the Liang dynasty . . . formed after the outline of the *Wen-hsüan* 文選." (Wylie loc. cit.).

F 25. *Ts'e-fu yüan-kuei* 冊府元龜. Taipei: Chung-hua, 1967. 20 vols.
Read Teng and Biggerstaff, p. 89; also Librarian of Congress Annual Report [B 15] vol. 1, p. 45. The term *yüan-kuei* originally meant "giant tortoise," of great value in olden times. The title therefore translates: "Great Treasure of the Hall of Books." It was compiled under

imperial auspices to contain information on government institutions and organization and is therefore a valuable source for students of pre-Sung government.

F 26. "Ts'e-fu yüan-kuei yin-te." 冊府元龜引得. Ch'en Hung-fei 陳鴻飛, in *Wen-hua t'u-shu-kuan hsüeh chi-k'an* 文華圖書館學季刊, 5.1:97-126 (March 1933).

In addition to the four books above, mention should also be made of:

F 27. Yü-hai 玉海. Wang Ying-lin 王應麟 (1223-1296). Taipei: Hua-wen, 1964. 8 vols.
The author, who lived into the Mongol era, is said to be the compiler of the *San-tzu-ching* 三字經.
Read Teng and Biggerstaff, pp. 92-93; also Librarian of Congress Annual Report [B 15] vol. 1, p. 45.

MING ENCYCLOPEDIAS

F 28. *Yung-lo ta-tien* 永樂大典. Peking: Chung-hua, 1960. 202 *chüan* in 20 cases. Taiwan repr: Shih-Chieh, 1962.
The third Ming emperor, Yung-lo 永樂 (reigned 1403-1424) intended to create, and probably achieved the greatest encyclopedia ever with the YLTT. The *Ssu-k'u t'i-yao* describes the history of its compilation. It is actually a dictionary of characters and phrases, arranged according to a classification based on 80 rhyme groups and explained by quotations from the classics and other literature. It had originally 22,937 *chüan* in 11,095 *ts'e*. Due to theft and war, there are now only 730 *chüan* in 202 *ts'e* extant.

Suggested Readings:

F 29. *Yung-lo ta-tien k'ao* 永樂大典考. Kuo Po-kung 郭伯恭, Changsha: Commercial Press, 1938; Taipei repr: Commercial Press, 1962 and 1967.

F 30. "Bibliography of the Chinese Imperial Collection." W. F. Mayers, in *China Review* 6:215-8 (1877/78) (with a translation of the *Ssu-k'u t'i-yao* description).

F 31. Librarian of Congress Annual Reports [B 15], vol. 1, pp. 144-152; vol. 2, pp. 515 and 523; vol. 3, pp. 1127-1128.

F 32. *British Museum Quarterly* 6:11-2, 97-8 (1932); 15:36-9 (1952); 26:30-3 (1962/63).

Other articles of interest:

New China Review 2:137-53 (1920).
Bodleian Library Record 3:198-200 (1950-51).
Tsing Hua Journal 2.2:93-115 (June 1961).
Chinese Literature 6:142-5 (1959).

CH'ING ENCYCLOPEDIAS

Several important encyclopedias or encyclopedic dictionaries were compiled under the Ch'ing, mostly on imperial command.

F 33. *Yüan-chien lei-han* 淵鑑類函. Compiled 1701 by an imperial committee. Taiwan edition: Hsin-hsing, 1960.
It makes use of earlier encyclopedias, e.g., *T'ang lei-han* 唐類函. The bulk of the work is made up of quotations from works up to the middle of the Ming dynasty. Read Teng and Biggerstaff, pp. 94-95; also W. F. Mayers [F 30], pp. 287-8.

F 34. *Ku-chin t'u-shu chi-ch'eng* 古今圖書集成. Completed 1926. Taiwan repr: Ting-wen, 1976.
A huge compilation in 32 sections, 6,109 subdivisions and 10,000 *chüan*. Read Teng and Biggerstaff, pp. 95-6; also W. Bauer [F 1], pp. 687-8.
The index compiled by Lionel Giles (London, 1911; Taipei repr, 1969) is an alphabetical list of topics, not titles of

books or authors. Entries selected by Giles "seem rather whimsical to the historian of science, who will find among them, for example, 'tiddly-winks' but not 'tides'." (Needham [D 50] vol. 1, p. 47).

F 35. *P'ei-wen yün-fu* 佩文韻府. Taiwan repr: Chung-hua, 1970; Commercial Press, 1970.

Read Teng and Biggerstaff, pp. 97-8. This is a compendium of literary phrases arranged according to the rhyme category of last word of the phrase quoted. There are 10,257 guide words under 106 rhyme categories. Citations under the binoms are listed in *ching, shih, tzu, chi* order (see p. 19) and within each section in chronological order. To find rhyme words, consult Giles' *Dictionary* [E 56], *Tz'u-yüan* [E 47], or *Trindex* [H 5]. There is no perceptible order within each rhyme word and searching is sometimes cumbersome.

The name *P'ei-wen yün-fu* derives from a hall in the imperial palace, the *P'ei-wen chai* 佩文齋. It was the "pavillon ou on honore les lettres" (Woo Kang [D 3], p. 57, footnote). See also W. Bauer [F 1], pp. 688-9, with the erroneous translation: "to carry the literature at the belt."

F 36. *P'ien-tzu lei-pien* 駢字類編. (Literary binoms systematically arranged). Taiwan repr: Hsüeh-sheng, n.d. This work groups binoms under 13 main headings: heaven and earth, time and calendar, mountains and rivers, etc., arranged according to the rhyme of the first of the two characters, with the second characters arranged topically, in the same order as the main groupings. Under each binom the quotations are arranged in the *ching, shih, tzu, chi* order. Read Teng and Biggerstaff, pp. 98-9; also F. W. Mayers [F 30] pp. 290-1.

[This, by the way was one of the 10 items received by the United States from China in 1869, see T. H. Tsien, "First Chinese-American Exchange of Publications," in *HJAS* 25:19-30 (1964/65). On this topic also see Chiang Fu-ts'ung in *West and East* 11.3:6-9 (March 1966); and Dorothy A. Day, "The Exchange of Publications: China and the United States." MA Thesis, University of Chicago, 1969.]

MODERN ENCYCLOPEDIAS

Unlike the Japanese, who have brought out several good encyclopedias which may also usefully be consulted on Chinese matters, the Chinese have not produced any noteworthy modern encyclopedias; check, for instance, *Chung-wen ts'an-k'ao yung-shu chih-nan* [D 9], p. 161.

F 37. *Yün-wu she-hui k'o-hsüeh ta tz'u-tien* 雲五社會科學大辭典. Taipei: Commercial Press, 1970-1971. 12 vols.
Useful as a dictionary of specialized terms. Read the General Preface 總目錄 in vol 1.

The Morohashi *Dictionary* [E 51] and its Chinese version, the *Chung-wen ta tz'u-tien* [E 52] are mentioned in the chapter on "Dictionaries." Wolfgang Bauer's comment on the Morohashi is that it is "certainly not a modern encyclopedia in the Western sense, but still shows the traditional compromise between dictionary, encyclopedia and anthology." (W. Bauer [F 1], p. 691).

Note: Information has been received recently that the Academy of Sciences at Peking is compiling a truly encyclopedic work, *Chung-kuo ta pai-k'o ch'üan-shu* 中國大百科全書 to be published in the near future.

G. Booklists/Library Catalogs/National Bibliographies

The booklists of imperial and ancient private libraries are important elements in the history of Chinese bibliography. The catologuing of the imperial libraries, initiated by Liu Hsiang and Liu Hsin and continued in the bibliographic sections of the official dynastic histories, has been mentioned earlier. When printing became more developed in the later Sung and especially in the Ming period, private book collections of considerable size began to be assembled. Their catalogs have assumed great historical value. Several of these old booklists have now become readily available in reprints from Taiwan, such as, the series *Shu-mu ts'ung-pien* 書目叢編, 1967– by the Kuang-wen shu-chü. For a description of the most important ancient book catalogs, see Teng and Biggerstaff, pp. 1-17 and the chapter on rare book catalogs, pp. 26-34. Also see the article "Bibliographie" (in German) by Walter Fuchs in *China-Handbuch* [C 17], pp. 154-8.

Other references:

For the Sung period:

G 1. *The Imperial Library in Southern Sung China, 1127-1279.* John H. Winkelman. Philadelphia: American Philosophical Society, 1974.

For the period T'ang to Ming:

G 2. "Scholarship, Book Production and Libraries in China, 618-1644." Wu Kwang-tsing. Unpublished Ph.D. Dissertation, University of Chicago, 1944.
See "Compilation of Annotated Catalogs" on pp. 134-7.

For the Ch'ing period:

G 3. *The Development of Chinese Libraries under the Ch'ing*

Dynasty, 1644-1911. Taam Cheuk-woon. Ph.D. Dissertation, University of Chicago, 1933.
Also contains information on Ming collections (pp. 7-13) and a useful bibliography (pp. 101-7).

The one book catalog that deserves particular mention in view of its practical usefulness is:

G 4. *Ssu-k'u ch'üan-shu tsung-mu t'i-yao* 四庫全書總目提要. Compiled by an imperial commission headed by Chi Yün 紀昀 and completed 1781. Taipei: T'ai-wan shang-wu, 1971. 5 volumes.
This work reproduces the descriptive notes from the catalog of the imperial collection. Read Teng and Biggerstaff, pp. 18-20; also the Librarian of Congress Annual Report for 1936 [B 15], Vol 2, p. 522. The 1971 Taiwan edition (in 5 volumes) also includes a four-corner index. As its complete title indicates: 合印四庫全書總目提要及四庫未收書目禁燬書目 it also contains (in vol. 5) other relevant booklists. The importance of this work lies in the fact that it was compiled by a commission of highly qualified scholars whose descriptions and evaluations of most of the works of Chinese traditional literature are usually accepted as authoritative. Read chapter on Chi Yün in Hummel's *Eminent Chinese* [L 27], vol. 1, pp. 121-2.

For equally practical considerations, two more recent Japanese booklists should be mentioned in this context:

G 5. *Naikaku Bunko kanseki bunrui mokuroku* 內閣文庫漢籍文類目錄. Tokyo: Naikaku Bunko, 1956.
Read Teng and Biggerstaff, p. 5.

G 6. *Kyōto Daigaku Jimbun Kagaku Kenkyujō kanseki bunrui mokuroku* 京都大學人文科學研究所漢籍文類目錄 Cf. [D 30] and read Teng and Biggerstaff, pp. 5-6.

These two catalogs list the holdings of the two best Japanese libraries as far as traditional Chinese literature is concerned. They are not annotated but are valuable tools for the verification of older Chinese works due to their comprehensiveness.

National Bibliographies

National bibliographies did not exist in Chinese before World War II. After the mainland and Taiwan became separate political entities, we have the following developments:

ON TAIWAN:

G 7. *Chung-hua min-kuo ch'u-pan t'u-shu mu-lu* 中華民國出版圖書目錄. National Central Library, Taipei, 1970- monthly with annual cumulations, also *hui-pien* 彙編 issued periodically, as e.g., for 1964, 1970, 1975.
Read review, with further data on annual trade bibliographies, by Robert Dunn of the *Chung-hua min-kuo ch'u-pan nien-chien* 中華民國出版年鑑 ("Publication Yearbook 1976") in the *Journal of Library and Information Science* 3.1:134-6 (April 1977).

For a review of the situation during the years 1949 to 1963 see Berton and Wu Guide, pp. 11-3, "National Bibliographies. Republic of China."

ON THE MAINLAND:

G 8. *Ch'üan-kuo hsin shu-mu* 全國新書目. National Library of Peking. 1951-1966, June 1972- irregular.
G 9. *Ch'üan-kuo tsung shu-mu* 全國總書目. National Library of Peking. 1949-1958, 1971- annual.

Both these publications are classified "for internal use," ostensibly to avoid people's disappointment or criticism because of unavailability (see Chan's article [G 10] below); they are therefore available only in copies smuggled out and copied in Hongkong or the United States.

References:

Berton and Wu Guide, chapter on "National Bibliographies," pp. 7-11.

Center for Chinese Research Materials Newsletter 15 (Jan. 1974), p. 4.

Read also:

G 10. "The New Era of Chinese Publishing and its Implications for Chinese Books Acquisitions." Y. S. Chan, in *Center for Chinese Research Materials Newsletter* 25:1-6 (March 1978).

H. Sinological Indexes and Concordances

Read Teng and Biggerstaff, p. 214.

Strangely enough, it was a Chinese admiral, Ts'ai T'ing-kan 蔡廷幹 (1861-1935), who compiled the first modern concordance to a Chinese classical text, namely:

H 1. *Lao-tzu tao te ching* 老子道德經. Ts'ai T'ing-kan. Shanghai, 1922.
The cover title is preceded by the words *Lao chieh Lao* 老解老 (Lao-tzu explained in Lao-tzu's terms). A full text of the work precedes the concordance which has characters arranged in order of their appearance in the text, with a stroke-count index at the end.

The production of sinological indexes on a larger scale was begun at Yenching University in Peking in the early thirties:

H 2. *Harvard-Yenching Institute Sinological Index Series*. Peking, Yenching University, 1931-
The editor-in-chief was William Hung 洪業 (1893-). The series covers a large section of the classical literature and has become an indispensable tool for locating phrases and single characters. Some of the indexes, for example, to the *Lun-yü, Meng-tzu,* and *Erh-ya,* have the full text of the works precede the index. Volume 4 of the supplemental series (1932) gives a historical overview and an explanation of the indexing method.

After closure of Yenching University due to the outbreak of the Pacific War, the French University in Peking, later in Paris, continued the work:

H 3. *Index de . . .*
Centre Franco-Chinois d'Etudes Sinologiques, Peking, 1943-

(Later: Centre d'Etudes Sinologiques de Pékin, Université de Paris)

Both these series have been reissued in Taiwan by Ch'eng Wen Publishing Company and by Chinese Materials Center. The explanatory foreword to these reprints by Glen W. Baxter is recommended reading. A full list of these sinological indexes and concordances is to be found in the appendix to this volume. The appendix also lists concordances, indexes, and other research aids published by Chinese Materials and Research Aids Service Center.

Similar indexes and concordances have also been published by other institutions; for example, by Ch'ung-chi College of the Chinese University of Hongkong; Kyoto Daigaku Toyoshi Kenkyukai, Kyoto; Daito Bunka Kenkyusha, Tokyo; and others.

A complete listing of indexes and concordances, to 1975, may be found in:

H 4. *Concordances and Indexes to Chinese Texts.* D. L. McMullen, comp. San Francisco: Chinese Materials Center, 1975.
This compilation lists and describes a vast number of concordances and indexes to Chinese texts. Read author's preface, pp. vii-ix.

A special purpose index which may be useful to the student is:

H 5. *Trindex* 三字典引得. Vernon Nash, comp. Index Press, Yenching University. Peiping, 1936. Taiwan Repr 1.
This is a combined index to the 13,848 characters in Giles' *Chinese-English Dictionary* [E 56], and to the same characters in *K'ang-hsi tzu-tien* [E 45] and the *P'ei-wen yün-fu* [F 35].

I. *Ts'ung-shu* and Their Indexes

The *ts'ung-shu* 叢書, usually referred to as "collectanea," are a peculiarly Chinese literary institution. They are collections of independent literary works which are published together under a collective title "in order that they may not be lost, or in order to give wider circulation to the writings of a particular locality, of one person, or of one family" (Teng and Biggerstaff, p. 66). The first work having "ts'ung-shu" in its title, the *Li-tse ts'ung-shu* 笠澤叢書 by Lu Kuei-meng 陸龜蒙 (d. ca. 878 A.D.), is, strictly speaking, not a *ts'ung-shu* because it is an anthology of the works of a single writer. (See Report of the Librarian of Congress for 1929-1930 [B 15] p. 351). It is only in the Sung dynasty that this genre became widespread, presumably due to greater facility in book production. With even more economical means in modern times, large sets of *ts'ung-shu* began to appear, particularly since the early twenties. However, while the traditional *ts'ung-shu* usually revealed much of the character and personality of the bookman who initiated it, the modern *ts'ung-shu* is motivated more by commercial considerations, some of them clearly imitating the German Reklam, the British Penguin books, and other publishers' series in paperback.

For a listing of some of the most important older *ts'ung-shu*, see:

I 1. "Ts'ung shu." Arthur W. Hummel, in *JAOS* 51:40-6 (1931).

Of the modern *ts'ung-shu* the most important examples are:

I 2. *Ssu-pu ts'ung-k'an* 四部叢刊 (*SPTK*). Shanghai: Commercial Press, 1920-1936. 2,100 *ts'e*, excluding the 24 histories issued independently.

Read the English introduction by Karl Lo to his *A Guide to the Ssu-pu ts'ung-k'an*, which is an index to authors, titles, and subjects. (Lawrence, Kansas, University of Kansas Libraries, 1965.) Also see the analysis of the works included in this *ts'ung-shu* in the 1922-23 Report of the Librarian of Congress [B 15], pp. 131-135. A review of the work is to be found in *T'u-shu-kuan-hsüeh chi-k'an* 圖書館學季刊 1.4:693-4 (December 1926).

I 3. *Ssu-pu pei-yao* 四部備要. Shanghai: Chung-hua, 1927-1935. 2,500 *ts'e*. Taiwan Repr: Chung-hua in 610 hardback volumes in western-style format, 1965-1966.
Read the English introduction by William C. Ju to his *A Guide to the Ssu-pu pei-yao*. (Taipei: Chung-hua shu-chü, 1971). Works in this collectanea are all selected from the imperial collection, the *Ssu-k'u ch'üan-shu* 四庫全書; see [I 5] below:

I 4. *Ts'ung-shu chi-ch'eng* 叢書集成. Shanghai: Commercial Press, 1935-1937. 4,100 *ts'e*.

I 5. *Ssu-k'u ch'üan-shu chen-pen* 四庫全書珍本. Taipei: Shang-wu, 1971-
Reproductions of books from the imperial collection at the Wen Yüan Ko palace, colorfully bound in western-style format.

I 6. *Pai-pu ts'ung-shu chi ch'eng* 百部叢書集成. Taipei: I-wen, 1967-
A collection of a large number of *ts'ung-shu* found on Taiwan.

Much of the value of *ts'ung-shu* lies in their function as a repository of otherwise unpublished, unavailable, or lost works. The huge volume of such items makes it impossible to list each item separately in the library catalogs, so that in many cases we must depend on special indexes to find these items hidden in *ts'ung-shu*. Over the years many attempts have been made to provide indexes to the contents of *ts'ung-shu* (see listing in Teng and Biggerstaff, 1950 edition), but all may now be considered superceded by the joint efforts of Shanghai libraries, see:

I 7. *Chung-kuo ts'ung-shu tsung-lu* 中國叢書總錄. Shanghai t'u-shu-kuan. Peking: Chung-hua, 1959-1962. 3 vols. "This is probably the most useful reference work compiled thus far by scholars in continental China; it is indispensable to every Chinese reference library" (Teng and Biggerstaff, p. 67).

A group connected with the College of Chinese Culture on Taiwan has reproduced the *Chung-kuo ts'ung-shu tsung-lu* under the title, *Ts'ung-shu ta tz'u-tien* 叢書大辭典. This title represents the first volume of the Shanghai index, but includes in addition, Yang Chia-lo's original compilation by that name and also a short essay (in Chinese) on the history of the *ts'ung-shu*. Taiwan has reproduced the second volume of the Shanghai index under the title, *Ts'ung-shu tzu-mu lei-pien* 叢書字目類編.

Independently useful Taiwan indexes to *ts'ung-shu* are:

I 8. *Ts'ung-shu tsung-mu hsü-pien* 叢書總目續編. Chuang Fang-jung 莊芳榮. Taipei: Te-hao, 1974.
An index to *ts'ung-shu* produced in Taiwan since 1949.

I 9. *T'ai-wan ko t'u-shu-kuan hsien-ts'un ts'ung-shu tzu-mu so-yin* 台灣各圖書館現存叢書子目索引. ("Title and Author Index to Ts'ung-shu in Taiwan Libraries") Wang Pao-hsien 王寶先. San Francisco: Chinese Materials Center, 1975. (CMC Research Aids Series, 7). Part I: Title Index; Part II: Author Index.

I 10. *Ts'ung-shu so-yin Sung wen tzu-mu* 叢書索引宋文子目. ("An Index to Sung Dynasty Titles Extant in *Ts'ung-shu*") Brian E. McKnight, comp. San Francisco, Chinese Materials Center, 1977. (CMC Research Aids Series, 15).

The Japanese have their own *ts'ung-shu* and *ts'ung-shu* indexes; the following is of interest in this context because it lists

Chinese *ts'ung-shu* in seven leading Japanese libraries:

I 11. *Kanseki sōsho shozai mokuroku* 漢籍叢書所在目錄 Tokyo: Toyo Bunko, Toyogaku Bunken Senta, 1965.

There have been attempts to group *ts'ung-shu* by subject matter, see:

I 12. "Ts'ung-shu". Arthur W. Hummel in *JAOS* 51:44-5 (1931).

I 13. *Kyoto Daigaku Jimbun Kagaku Kenkyujo kanseki bunrui mokuroku* 京都大學人文科學研究所漢籍文類目錄. See [D 30]. Note the *ts'ung-shu* section in the table of contents!

Suggested additional readings on the *ts'ung-shu*:

I 14. "Ts'ung-shu chih yüan-liu lei-pieh chi ch'i pien so-yin fa" 叢書之源流類別及其編索引法 Wang Kuo-yüan 汪國垣, in *Mu-lu-hsüeh yen-chiu* 目錄學研究. Shanghai: Commercial Press, 1955, pp. 95-126.

I 15. "Ts'ung-shu k'an-k'o yüan-liu k'ao" 叢書刊刻源流考. Hsien Kuo-chen 謝國楨, in *Ming Ch'ing pi-chi t'an-ts'ung* 明清筆記談叢. Peking: Chung-hua, 1962, pp. 202-41.

J. Chinese History and Government Institutions.

History has always been much more of an intellectual preoccupation in China than in Western countries. A sense of history pervades all fields of thought, be it in education, philosophical inquiry, or practical politics. The volume of records, descriptive and critical literature, is correspondingly large. However, since the "Far East" has come appreciably closer to the rest of the world, particularly since World War II, the bibliographic coverage of Chinese history has also greatly expanded. In the following we shall limit ourselves to history proper, prehistory will be covered in the chapter on ARCHEOLOGY.

Recommended introductory reading:

J 1. "Far Eastern History." Ernst Wolff, in *Library Trends* 15.4:745-58 (April 1967).

J 2. *Essays on the Sources of Chinese History*. Donald D. Leslie, Colin Mackerras, Wang Gungwu, eds. Columbia, South Carolina, University of South Carolina Press, 1975. Previously published in Australia in 1973.
A collection of essays on the sources "that can help toward an understanding of Chinese history in general (especially those dealing with traditional China)" (Preface, p. v). Especially valuable are the bibliographies following the various chapters.

J 3. *The Cambridge History of China*. Denis Twitchett and John K. Fairbank, general eds. Cambridge, England, Cambridge University Press, 1978-
Recommended for "introductory scanning," rather than "reading" since this will be a work of 14 volumes when completed. Each volume has a bibliographic essay and a huge bibliography of the period treated. Volume 10: Late Ch'ing, 1800-1911, Part I, was the first to be pub-

lished. Read the substantial review of this volume by Prof. Ping-ti Ho in JAS 39.1:133-6 (Nov. 1979).

COMPREHENSIVE HISTORICAL BIBLIOGRAPHIES

In addition to the general bibliographies of world history which include coverage of China, such as the *Foreign Affairs Bibliography* or the *International Bibliography of Historical Sciences*, the student should also be aware of the following which focus on Chinese history or segments of Chinese history:

J 4. *Chinese History, a Bibliographic Review.* Charles O. Hucker. Service Center for Teachers of History of the American Historical Association, Washington, D.C., 1958. A short (forty-two pages) very readable introduction to the field "to acquaint secondary-school teachers with materials available." (Introduction, p. 1).

J 5. *Chung-kuo li-shih yen-chiu kung-chü shu (kao-pen)* 中國歷史研究工具書(稿本). ("Research Tools to Chinese History, an Annotated Bibliography") Tseng Ying-ching 曾影靖. Hongkong: Lung-men, 1968.
Although never revised from "draft" format and lacking an index, this is a highly commendable compilation of all the reference works in the field. Students should read the foreword (also in English) and scan the table of contents.

J 6. *Historians of China and Japan.* W. G. Beasley and E. G. Pulleyblank, eds. London: Oxford University Press, 1961. A collection of excellent essays on Chinese historiography written by experts in their particular historical specialization (see list of contents) providing a useful bibliographic survey. Also read the substantial review by A. Feuerwerker and R. F. Hatchett in *JAS* 21.3:393-4 (May 1962).

J 7. *Premodern China; a Bibliographical Introduction.* Chang

Chun-shu. Center for Chinese Studies, University of Michigan, Ann Arbor, 1971. 183 pp.

J 8. "Early Chinese History: The State of the Field." Hsu Cho-yun in *JAS* 38.3:453-475 (May 1979).

J 9. *Modern China; a Bibliographic Guide to Chinese Works 1898-1937.* John K. Fairbank and K. C. Liu. Cambridge, Mass.: Harvard University Press, 1950.

J 10. *Japanese Studies of Modern China: A Bibliographic Guide to Historical and Social Science Research on the 19th and 20th Century.* John K. Fairbank and Masataka Banno. Tokyo: Tuttle, 1955.

J 11. *Japanese Studies of Modern China Since 1955: A Bibliographical Guide to Historical and Social Science Research on the 19th and 20th Century.* N. Kamachi, John F. Fairbank, Chūzō Ichiko. Cambridge, Mass.: Harvard University Press, 1975.

J 12. *Research Materials on 20th Century China: an Annotated List of Center for Chinese Research Materials Publications.* P. K. Yu, ed. Center for Chinese Research Materials, Washington, D.C., 1975.

Read the foreword by F. W. Mote and note the table of contents.

J 13. *Chung-kuo chin-tai-shih ts'an-k'ao shu-mu ch'u-pien* 1842-1919 中國近代史參考書目初編 . Shanghai: Hua-tung shih-fan ta-hsüeh, 1962.

A modest compilation of only ninety-three pages, but covering a difficult to chart period in Chinese history.

J 14. *Bücherkunde zur chinesischen Geschichte, Kultur und Gesellschaft.* Reiner Hoffmann. Munich, Germany: Weltforum Verlag, 1973.

Particularly interesting for its short annotations and for its copious references to review articles on many of the books listed.

ENCYCLOPEDIAS AND DICTIONARIES OF CHINESE HISTORY.

For general information on Chinese history recent articles in general encyclopedias such as the *Encyclopaedia Britannica* and the *Encyclopedia Americana* may be consulted. However, there is as yet no special encyclopedia of Chinese history with an acceptable standard of quality and coverage. With that reservation in mind, the following are mentioned:

J 15. *Chung-hua li-shih ti-li ta tz'u-tien* 中華歷史地理大辭典. Chang Ch'in 章嶔. Originally published in 1913. Taipei Repr: Hsin-wen-feng, 1974. 2 vols.

J 16. *Li-shih hsiao tz'u-tien* 歷史小辭典. Chou Mu-chai 周木齋. Taipei: Hua-lien, 1968.

J 17. *Li-shih-hsüeh* 歷史學. Fang Hao 方豪. Taipei: Commercial Press, 1970.
(Yün-wu she-hui k'o-hsüeh ta tz'u-tien 雲五社會科學大辭典, vol. 12).

Some of the Japanese historical dictionaries will perhaps be found more useful:

J 18. *Ajia rekishi jiten* アジア歷史辭典. Tokyo: Heibonsha, 1959-1962. 10 vols.

J 19. *Tōyō rekishi daijiten* 東洋歷史辭典. Tokyo: Heibonsha, 1937-1939. 9 vols.

Mentioned here more because of its name than contents:

J 20. *Dictionary of Chinese History*. Michael Dillon. London: Frank Cass, 1979.
With a scope of "pre-history to the end of 1977" in only 240 23-cm pages, this work attemps too much, but it provides a "quick and easy reference to the names and terms . . . in English-language works on China" (see preface). No bibliography or bibliographic references.

CHRONOLOGIES

Although the field of historical encyclopedias is not well represented, there is no lack of chronologies and chronological tables of events covering all periods of Chinese history up to the present. Most of the reliable dictionaries, such as *Giles* [E 56], *Mathews* [E 57], *Tz'u-hai* [E 48] and *Tz'u-yüan* [E 47], will have such chronologies as prefatory or appended material. Some chronologies are combined with calendar concordances (see p. 87) or with lists of imperial reign names (see p. 91).

Suggested introductory reference: Teng and Biggerstaff, pp. 195-203. The following is a short list of chronologies deserving particular mention:

J 21. *Chung-kuo ta-shih nien-piao* 中國大事年表. Ch'en Ch'ing-ch'i 陳慶麒. Shanghai: Commercial Press, 1934. Reprinted Taipei, 1963; Hongkong, 1964.
Scope: early history to 1932.

J 22. *Chung-kuo chin-tai-shih shih-chi* 中國近代史事記. Ch'i-lin shih-fan ta-hsüeh Chung-kuo chin-tai-shih chiao-yen-shih. Shanghai: Shang-hai jen-min, 1961.
Scope: 1514-1949. Dates in Western and cyclical notations.

J 23. *Chung-kuo li-tai ti-wang p'u-hsi hui-pien* 中國歷代帝王譜系彙編. Chia Hu-ch'en 賈虎臣. Taipei: Cheng-chung, 1966.
"Imperial rulers in successive dynasties. Also succinct brief summary of each emperor's merits and demerits" (Teng and Biggerstaff, p. 200).

J 24. *Kuo-shih nien-piao ssu-chung* 國史年表四種. Taipei: Shih-chieh shu-chü, 1963.
A reprint of four older important works, (cf. Teng and Biggerstaff, p. 195, footnote 1), namely:

J 25. *Li-tai ti-wang nien piao* 歷代帝王年表. Ch'i Chao-nan 齊召南. Preface 1777.

J 26. *Ming nien piao* 明年表. Juan Fu 阮福. Preface 1824.

J 27. *Ch'ing nien piao* 清年表. Hsiao I-shan 蕭一山.

J 28. *Chung-hua min-kuo nien piao* 中華民國年表. Yü Li-lin 余戾林. (Originally Ch'eng-tu, 1946.)

J 29. *Chung-kuo ta-shih chi* 中國大事記. Center for Chinese Research Materials, Washington, D.C., 1973.
Reprint in six volumes of the chronologies found in the *Tung-fang tsa-chih* 東方雜誌 and Kuo T'ing-yi's chronology. (*Chin-tai Chung-kuo shih shih jih chih* 近代中國史事日誌. Kuo T'ing-i 郭廷以 [1903-1975]. Taipei: Cheng-chung, 1963. 2 vols.) Read the introduction.

J 30. *Chung-hua min-kuo ta shih-chi* 中華民國大事記. Kao Yin-tsu 高蔭祖 and Liu Shih-ch'ang 劉世昌. Taipei: Shih-chieh, 1957.
Scope: 1911-1946. Reviewed in Teng and Biggerstaff, p. 198. Claims to have used 127 sources as reference.

J 31. *Chung Jih Han pai-nien ta-shih chi* 中日韓百年大事記. Ch'en Ku-t'ing 陳固亭. Taipei: T'ai-wan, 1971.
Scope: 1866-1965. Has Japanese year designations parallel with Western and Chinese.

J 32. *Chung-kuo kuo-min-tang pa-shih nien ta-shih nien-piao* 中國國民黨八十年大事年表 KMT Party History Committee, Taipei, 1974.
Scope: 1895-1974.

J 33. *Chung-shan ch'u-shih hou Chung-kuo liu-shih nien ta-shih chi* 中山出世後中國六十年大事記. Li Chien-nung 李劍農 comp. Shanghai: T'ai-p'ing-yang, 1929.
Scope: 1866-1928.

J 34. *Tōhō nempyō* 東方年表. Fujishima Tatsuro 藤島達郎 and Nogami Shunjo 野上俊靜. Kyoto: Heirakuji Shoten, 1955. Taiwan reprint.
An East Asia chronology which Endymion Wilkinson calls "most convenient" [C 8], p. 26).

J 35. *Kaihō nippō kiji mokuroku* 解放日報記事目錄 Tokyo: Kindai Chugoku Kenkyu Iinkai, 1967-1968. 4 vols.

Scope: 1941-1947. See N. Kamachi, *Japanese Studies of Modern China* [J 11], p. 266.

J 36. *The Rulers of China, 221 B.C.-A.D. 1949: Chronological Tables*. Arthur Christopher Moule. New York: Praeger, 1957.
Read review by H. H. Frankel in *JAS* 18.1:121-2 (November 1958).

J 37. *Chronological Tables of the Chinese Dynasties*. Theodore Wang (Wang Tso-t'ing). Shanghai: Shanghai Printing Co., 1902. Repr: Taipei, 1976.

J 38. *Sung tai shih nien-piao* 宋代史年表. Tokyo: Japan Committee for the Sung Project, 1974. 2 vols.

J 39. *Chronology of the People's Republic of China, 1949-1972*. Peter P. Cheng. Totowa, N. J.: Littlefield, 1972.

CALENDAR CONCORDANCES

The determination of Chinese historical dates is complicated by the use of the sexagenary system (*liu-shih hua-chia* 六十花甲) of year and day notations in traditional Chinese historiography. These notations are formed by combining a series of ten characters, the ten celestial stems (*t'ien-kan* 天干), with another series, the twelve earthly branches (*ti-chih* 地支), to form 60 combinations. Conversion of these sexagenary date-codes into the corresponding years of our Western calendar system is usually done by means of tables. Such tables will be found in the larger dictionaries, or in the chronological tables. For more complicated conversions the use of special conversion tables is necessary.

Suggested introductory reading:

J 40. "Sexagenary cycles." Joseph Needham, *Science and Civilization in China*. Cambridge, Eng., Cambridge University Press, vol. 3 (1959) pp. 396-8.

Actual conversion tables are:

J 41. *Liang-ch'ien nien lai Chung Hsi li tui-chao piao* 兩千年來中西曆對照表. ("A Sino-Western Calendar for Two Thousand Years"). Hsieh Chung-san 薛仲三 and Ou-yang I 歐陽頤. Rev. ed. Hongkong: Commercial Press, 1961. Reprinted by Krisha Press, New York 1974.
The most convenient one but useful only after a careful study of its explanatory introduction (Also read Teng and Biggerstaff, p. 194).

J 42. *Concordances des chronologies néoméniques, chinoise et européenne*. P. Hoang. Shanghai: Zikawai, 1910. 2nd rev. and enlarged ed., with an informative English introduction, Taichung: Kuang-ch'i, 1968.

J 43. *Chin-shih Chung Hsi shih jih tui-chao piao* 近代中西史日對照表. Cheng Ho-sheng 鄭鶴聲. Nanking: Kuo-li pien-i-kuan, 1936. Taipei repr, 1966.
A handy conversion table covering the years from 1516 (arrival of Rafael Perestrello in China) to 1941, with a special calendar for the Taiping kingdom (1851-1865).

J 44. *Chung Hsi Hui shih jih li* 中西回史日曆. Ch'en Yüan 陳垣. Original preface 1925. Rev. ed. Peking: Chung-hua, 1962. Taipei repr: Yi-wen, 1972.
See Teng and Biggerstaff, pp. 192-3.

Those gifted in mental arithmetic may consider one of the simple (?) conversion methods:

J 45. "A simple method for mental conversion of a year expressed in cyclical characters to the corresponding year in the Western calendar." N. Sivin, in *Japanese Studies in the History of Science,* 4:132-4 (1965).

J 46. "Quick conversion of Chinese sexagenary year designations into Western dates." Alvin P. Cohen, in *Journal of the Chinese Language Teachers Association* 11.3:194-8 (October 1976).

J 47. "Formulae for the respective conversion of Chinese and Western dates." John Marney, in *Journal of the Chinese Lang. Teachers Assoc.* 12.1:143-5 (May 1977).

J 48. *Tōdai no koyomi* 唐代の暦. Hiraoka Takeo 平岡武夫. Kyoto: Kyoto University, 1954. Series: *Todai kenkyū no shiori*, vol. 1. 唐代研究のつね
Limited to the T'ang dynasty.

J 49. *Chung-kuo chin-tai shih li piao* 中國近代史曆表. Jung Meng-yüan 榮孟源. Hongkong: Commercial Press, 1962.
Most convenient for Ch'ing and Post-Ch'ing dynasty dates; covers 1830-1949.

THE DYNASTIC HISTORIES

The backbone of traditional Chinese history is the series of official, or standard, histories (*cheng shih* 正史) which were usually compiled for each dynasty by the subsequent one. The *Shih-chi* 史記 by Ssu-ma Ch'ien 司馬遷 (1st century B.C.) was the prototype for official history. A convenient table of all the twenty-four standard histories is on p. 16 of Wylie's *Notes* [C 13]. Their number is sometimes given as twenty-five, if the *Hsin Yüan shih* 新元史 by K'o Shao-min 柯劭忞 (completed 1920) is added.

The history of the Manchu dynasty, prepared at Mukden (Shenyang) in the late twenties, has remained a draft: the *Ch'ing shih kao* 清史稿. Objections to its pro-Ch'ing bias have been raised. Due to alleged defects, it is generally not included in the count of standard histories. A Taiwan compilation, the *Ch'ing-shih* 清史 published in 1961 by the National Defense College in 8 volumes is "unfortunately full of errors" (Wilkinson [C 8], p. 85). It was revised and reprinted in the Jen-shou edition of standard histories (see below).

The best known edition of standard histories was published in the thirties by the Shanghai Commercial Press in its series *Ssu-pu ts'ung-k'an* [I 2]. It is generally referred to as the *Po-na-pen* edition due to the fact that it was collated from various originals (百衲本 = edition put together like the patched robe of a mendicant monk). A new punctuated edition has been published by the Chung-hua shu-chü, Peking, in 135 volumes, completed in 1977. On Taiwan a facsimile reproduction of earlier editions was published, unpunctuated, as the Jen-shou edition 仁壽本二十五史 in 934 volumes by a special agency organized for that purpose, the Erh-shih-wu shih pien k'an kuan 二十五史編刊館 1955-1956. The mainland punctuated edition has also been reprinted on Taiwan.

Suggested reading:

J 50. "Standard histories, Han to Sui." K. H. J. Gardiner, in *Essays of the Sources for Chinese History* [J 2] pp. 42-52.

J 51. "Some comments on the later standard histories." Wang Gungwu, in *Essays on the Sources for Chinese History* [J 2] pp. 53-63.

J 52. "Notes on the Dynastic Histories." L. C. Goodrich, in *Topics in Chinese History*, ed. by Yang Lien-sheng. Cambridge, Mass.: Harvard University Press, 1950, pp. 32-8.

J 53. "The Organization of Chinese Official Historiography: Principles and Methods of the Standard Histories from the T'ang through the Ming Dynasty." Yang Lien-sheng, in *Historians of China and Japan* [J 6] pp. 44-59.

On the *Ch'ing shih kao* in particular read:

J 54. "Chao Er-sun 趙爾巽." In Boorman's *Dictionary of Republican China* [L 30] vol. 1, pp. 141-2.
Chao Wa, the editor-in-chief of the *Ch'ing shih kao*.

J 55. "A comparison of the various editions of the *ch'ing shih kao*." C. H. Peake, in *T'oung Pao* 35:354-63 (1940).

J 56. "The *Ch'ing shih kao*, a bibliographical summary." Thurston Griggs, in *HJAS* 18:105-23 (1955).

Of value for biographical research are the extensive biographical sections (*chuan* 傳 or *lieh chuan* 列傳) of the dynastic histories. For indexes to these see:

J 57. *Erh-shih-wu shih jen-ming so-yin* 二十五史人名索引. Shanghai: K'ai-ming, 1935. Reprinted in Peking and Taiwan. Taiwan Repr: K'ai-ming, 1965.
See Teng and Biggerstaff, p. 178.

J 58. *Shih-chi jen-ming so-yin* 史記人名索引. Chung Hua 鍾華. Peking: Chung-hua, 1977. Taipei Repr: Chiu-ssu, 1979.
Indexes by four-corner and stroke count to the names of all persons mentioned in the *Shih-chi*, the first of the standard histories.

REIGN NAMES 年號 AND TABOO CHARACTERS 諱字

A further complication in Chinese historiography is the age-old custom of the imperial rulers of China to assign auspicious designations to the years of their reign—some for the entire duration of their reign, some changing the reign designations after a number of years. In Western usage, reign names are sometimes used as if they were the emperor's names, so we speak of Emperor Kanghsi or Emperor Chienlung, but in traditional Chinese writings it is more common that the emperor is referred to by his honorific, or posthumous name (*shih* 謚 or *miao hao* 廟號 temple name), in this case, Ch'ing Sheng-tsu and Ch'ing Kao-tsung (thus also Library of Congress main entries).

Suggested readings:

J 59. *Chinese Traditional Historiography*. Charles Sidney Gardner. Cambridge, Mass.: Harvard University Press, 1961, p. 72.

J 60. "What's in a reign name? The uses of history and philology." Mary C. Wright, in *JAS* 18:103-6 (1958/59).

J 61. "Chinese Reign Names—Words or Nonsense Syllables?" Edward H. Schafer, in *Wennti* (Yale University) 3:33-40 (July 1952).

J 62. "Era names and Zeitgeist." Arthur F. Wright and Edward Fagan, in *Etudes Asiatiques* 5:113-21 (1951).
This is a review of Ichimura Sanjiro's article "Nengo ni arawaretaru jidai shisō" in *Shigaku zasshi* 39 (1928), but with much substance in and of itself.

J 63. "Communication to editors" (Subject: reign names). Edward H. Schafer in *JAS* 18:431-2 (1959/59).

J 64. "The Origin of an Éra." Edward H. Schafer in *JAOS* 85:543-50 (1965).

For tables of reign names, see chronologies in most of the larger dictionaries, also calendar concordances and chronologies, especially those of Ch'en Yüan [J 44], Hsieh Chung-san [J 41] and Chia Hu-ch'en [J 23]. Hsieh Chung-san's concordance has an alphabetically arranged index to the Chinese reign names in table 16. In Chia Hu-ch'en's chronology there is an index of reign names by stroke count. See also:

J 65. *Chung-kuo li-tai nien-hao so-yin* 中國歷代年號索引. Wang Hung-sheng 汪宏聲. Shanghai: K'ai-ming, 1936. Taipei Repr: Wen-hai, 1972.
Chronologically arranged with an index arranged by stroke count.

J 66. *Chung Hsi tui-chao li-tai chi-nien t'u-piao* 中西對照歷代紀年圖表. Wan Kuo-ting 萬國鼎. Original preface 1927. Taipei: Commercial Press, 1963; also reprinted in Hongkong under the title: *Chung-kuo li-shih chi-nien piao* 中國歷史紀年表, in 1958, and again in 1962.

Taboo Characters

The taboo on writing or mentioning personal names applied in the case of members of the older generation of one's family, of widely venerated personalities, such as Confucius and Mencius, but particularly in the case of emperors of the contemporary dynasty. The taboo required either omission of the character, leaving a blank space, or an orthographic change, such as the omission of one stroke, e.g., 𤣥 for 玄, or substitution of another form, e.g., 湻 for 淳, or of another character, e.g., 怡 for 儀. The practice obviously produces a certain amount of confusion. Its only advantage is that it can, in some instances, facilitate the dating of documents and the establishment of their authenticity.

Recommended readings:

J 67. *Chinese Traditional Historiography*. Charles Sidney Gardner. Cambridge, Mass.: Harvard University Press, 1961, pp. 81-5.
In footnote 12, p. 84, Gardner cites an article in French by A. Vissiere and a German article by E. Haenisch, which are recommended for further study, particularly the table in the latter.

J 68. *Li-tai hui-tzu p'u* 歷代諱字譜. Chang Wei-hsiang 張惟驤. 1928.
Described in Teng and Biggerstaff, pp. 137-8.

J 69. *Shih-hui chü-li* 史諱舉例. Ch'en Yüan 陳垣. Peking: Chung-hua, 1956 and 1962. Taipei Repr: Wen-shih-che, 1978.
Originally published in *Yen-ching hsüeh-pao* 4 (1928). Revised in later editions. Considered "an excellent general study of taboo names throughout history," see Gardner [J 67].

GOVERNMENT INSTITUTIONS AND OFFICIAL TITLES

(Note: The researcher in this area might find it helpful to know that libraries following the Library of Congress subject headings will have their material cataloged under the headings "Civil service–China" and "China–Officials and employees.")

Primary sources for premodern political and social institutions are mostly contained in encyclopedic works designated as *shih-t'ung* 史通 or *hui-yao* 會要, to which may be added the *Ts'e-fu yüan-kuei* encyclopedia mentioned earlier [F 25]. On the *shih-t'ung* and *hui-yao* the student is urged to read Teng and Biggerstaff's excellent description on pp. 107-19.

Further suggested readings:

J 70. *Chinese Traditional Historiography*. Charles Sidney Gardner. Cambridge, Mass.: Harvard University Press, 1961. Chapter VII "Formal Classification," pp. 86-105.

J 71. "L'Histoire comme guide de la pratique bureaucratique." Etienne Balazs, in *Historians of China and Japan*, ed. by Beasley and Pulleyblank [J 6], pp. 78-94.

General Works

Western language works that provide an overall view of Chinese political institutions, and may, at the same time, provide appropriate glossaries of institutional terms, include:

J 72. *Studies of Governmental Institutions in Chinese History*. John Lyman Bishop, ed. Cambridge, Mass.: Harvard University Press, 1968. (Harvard-Yenching Institute studies, 23).
Reproduces seven studies formerly published in the *HJAS*.

J 73. *Studies in Chinese Institutional History*. Yang Lien-sheng, ed. Cambridge, Mass.: Harvard University Press, 1961. (Harvard-Yenching Institute studies, 20).
Reproduces nine articles formerly published in the *HJAS*.

J 74. *The Chinese Civil Service: Career open to Talent*? Johanna M. Menzel, ed. Boston: Heath, 1963.
Reviewed by Ch'en Ch'i-yün in *Revue Bibliographique de Sinologie* 9:48 (1971): "The editor's introduction and bibliographic suggestions are more comprehensive and cover a much wider scope than those of the selected articles," which are 13 essays by different authors on traditional Chinese civil service systems.

J 75. "L'organisation definitive du mandarinat." Etienne Balazs, in *Histoire et Institutions de la Chine Ancienne*. Henri Maspero and Etienne Balazs. Paris: Presses Universitaires de France, 1976, pp. 172-98.

J 76. *Historians of China and Japan*, see [J 6].

Of Chinese and Japanese works, the following are recommended for information on official titles and explanation of offices in traditional China:

J 77. *Li-tai chih-kuan piao* 歷代制官表. Chi Yün 紀昀 and others. Shanghai: Commercial Press, 1936. For publication details and other editions see Teng and Biggerstaff, p. 200.

J 78. *Chung-kuo wen-kuan chih-tu shih* 中國文官制度史. Yang Shu-fan 楊樹藩. Taipei: San-min, 1976.

J 79. *Shina kansei hattatsu shi* 支那官制發達史. Wada Sei 和田清 ed. Tokyo: Kyuko Shoin, 1942. Reprinted Taipei, 1973.
Scope: up to the Yüan dynasty. Contains a rich bibliography of Chinese and Japanese source material.

By Historical Periods (Dynasties)

The following is a listing of detailed studies of Chinese government institutions and offices for particular historical periods (dynasties).

HAN 漢:

J 80. *Official Titles of the Former Han Dynasty*. Rafe De-Crespigny. Canberra: Centre of Oriental Studies, 1967.

J 81. *Records of the Han Administration*. Michael Loewe. Cambridge, Eng: University Press, 1967. 2 vols.
Volume 1 contains "Glossary of Terms."

J 82. *Crisis and Conflict in Han China 104* B.C.-A.D. *9*. Michael Loewe. London: Allen and Unwin, 1974.
Pp. 307-14: "The Institutions of Han Government."

J 83. *Ssu-ma Ch'ien, Grand Historian of China*. Burton Watson. New York: Columbia University Press, 1958. Glossary on pp. 247-65.

J 84. *Han-shih ts'ai-liao yü Han-shih lun-chu tsung-ho mu-lu* 漢史材料與漢史論著綜合目錄. Ma Hsien-hsing 馬先醒. Yang-ming-shan: College of Chinese Culture, 1970.
See in particular the chapters 政治制度 and 官制地方行政系統.

WEI, CHIN, NAN-PEI CH'AO 魏晉南北朝:

J 85. *Wei Chin Nan-pei ch'ao shih yen-chiu lun-wen shu-mu yin-te* 魏晉南北朝史研究論文書目引得. Kuang Li-an 鄺利安. Taipei: Chung-hua, 1971.

T'ANG 唐:

J 86. *Traité des fonctionnaires et traité de l'armée*. Robert Des Rotours. Leiden: Brill, 1947-48. 2 vols. Repr. 1.
Translations of parts of the *Hsin T'ang shu* 新唐書.

J 87. *Financial Administration under the T'ang Dynasty*. Denis C. Twitchett. Cambridge, Eng.: Cambridge University Pr., 1970.
Glossary on pp. 369-80.

J 88. *Quellen zur Rechtsgeschichte der T'ang-Zeit*. Karl Bünger. Peking: Catholic University, 1946. (Monumenta Serica Monograph Series, 9).
Glossary of officials and titles (in German).

SUNG 宋:

J 89. *Les fonctionnaires des Song: Index des Titres*. Chang Fu-jui. Paris: Mouton, 1962.

J 90. *Civil Service in Early Sung China*. Edward A. Kracke. Cambridge, Mass.: Harvard University Press, 1953.
See in particular pp. 229-35: "The protocol list of 1038."

J 91. "Materiaux de recherches sur la periode Song." Yves

Hervouet, in *Bulletin de liaison pour les études chinoises en Europe* 6.4:16-32 (1973).

J 92. *Soshi shokukanshi sakuin* 宋史職官志索引. Saeki Tomi 佐伯富. Kyoto: Kyoto Daigaku Toyoshi Kenkyukai, 1963.

YÜAN 元:

J 93. *Un Code des Yüan*. Paul Ratchnevsky. Vol. 1, Paris: Leroux, 1937; vol. 2, Paris: Presses Universitaires de France, 1972; vol. 3, Paris: Press Universitaires de France, 1977 (with Francoise Aubin).
Indispensable for the study of Yuan institutions; vol. 2 contains a bibliography (pp. 185-97) of which the latest item is dated 1968. Vol. 1 is the index which lists items in Chinese characters with French translations.

MING 明:

J 94. "Governmental Organization of the Ming Dynasty." Charles O. Hucker, in *Studies of Governmental Institutions in Chinese History* [J 72].
This is the reprinted but newly indexed article originally published in *HJAS* 21 (1958).

J 95. *An Introduction to the Sources of Ming History*. Wolfgang Franke. Kuala Lumpur: University of Malaya, 1968.
Read the introduction to Section 6, "Works on Political Institutions."

CH'ING 清;

J 96. *Present Day Political Organization of China*. H. S Brunnert and V. V. Hagelstrom. Rev. ed. Shanghai: Kelly and Walsh, 1912. Repr 1.

J 97. *Ch'ing Administrative Terms*. E-tu Zen Sun. Cambridge, Mass.: Harvard University Press, 1961.
A translation of the *Liu-pu ch'eng-yü chu chieh* 六部成語

注解 (The Six Boards with Explanatory Notes), an anonymous work of 1742.

J 98. *The Internal Organization of Ch'ing Bureaucracy*. Thomas Albert Metzger. Cambridge, Mass.: Harvard University Press, 1973.

J 99. *Legal Institutions in Manchu China: A Sociological analysis*. Sybille Van Der Sprenkel. London: Athlone Press, 1962; New York: Humanities Press, 1966.

J 100. *The Chinese Government*. William Frederick Mayers. Shanghai: American Presbyterian Mission Press; London: Trübner, 1878. Repr 1.

REPUBLICAN CHINA 民國:

In addition to the two basic reference works previously mentioned, namely Andrew Nathan's *Modern China* [C 7] and Charles O. Hucker's *China; a Critical Bibliography* [C 4], there are:

J 101. *The Political Institutions of Modern China*. William L. Tung. The Hague: M. Nijhoff, 1968.
The scope of this work extends from the Ch'ing to the PRC.

J 102. *Hsin-hai i-hou shih-ch'i nien chih-kuan nien piao* 辛亥以後十七年職官年表. Liu Shou-lin 劉壽林. Peking: Chung-hua, 1966. Hongkong repr, 1974. Taiwan repr: Wen-hai, 1974.
The scope of this work is 1912-1928.

J 103. "Sources on Kuomintang and Republican China." Stephen Fitzgerald, in *Essays on the Sources for Chinese History* [J 2] pp. 229-40.

J 104. *Chinese Historiography on the Revolution of 1911: A Critical Survey and a Selected Bibliography*. Winston Hsieh. Stanford, Calif.: Hoover Institutions Press, 1975.

PEOPLE'S REPUBLIC 人民 :

J 105. "Constitution and Government." Franklin W. Houn, in *China, a Handbook* [C 15], pp. 221-39.

J 106. *The Political Institutions of Modern China* [J 101]. Particularly valuable are chapters, X, "The Communist Party in Power," and XI, "Fundamental Laws of the PRC"; also the excellent bibliography on pp. 380-93, all items in which are pre-Cultural Revolution writings.

J 107. *Developments on the PRC: A Selected Bibliography.* Patricia Blair, comp. Overseas Development Council, Washington, D.C., 1976 (ODC Occasional Paper no. 8).

J 108. "Sources on the History of the Chinese Communist Party." Hsüeh Chün-tu, in *Essays on the Sources for Chinese History* [J 2], pp. 241-50.
A useful bibliography through 1971.

J 109. "Sources on the Chinese People's Republic." Bill Brugger, in *Essays on the Sources for Chinese History* [J 2], pp. 251-65.

J 110. *Directory of Central Officials in the PRC, 1968-1978.* Malcolm Lamb. Canberra: Australian National University 1978. (Australian National University. Contemporary China Papers, 10 revised).

J 111. *Directory of Selected Scientific Institutions in Mainland China.* Stanford, Calif.: Hoover Institution Press, 1970. The introduction mentions (on p. x) four earlier works also relevant to this subject.

J 112. *PRC: A Bibliography of Research Aids and Primary Sources in English.* Chang, Yeen-mei Wu. East Asia Library, University of Washington, Seattle, February 1979. Mimeographed. 23 pp.
A handy and useful bibliography based on the holdings of the East Asia Library.

Organizational charts and directories of officials and government organizations are also occasionally issued by the U.S.

Central Intelligence Agency, updating information on the changing pattern of administrative organization in the PRC.

For the Republic of China (Taiwan):

On offices, government institutions and English equivalents for related terms, see English editions of the Taiwan-published *China Yearbooks* [Q 4].

HISTORICAL PERIODICALS/NEWSLETTERS

While periodicals are discussed in general in section P, we wish to point out here a fairly recent development, namely the appearance of newsletters that provide information on contemporary scholarship concerning a single period of Chinese history. At the time, there are the following newsletters of this type:

Early China (formerly *Pre-Han China*), Berkeley, California, 1975-
Nan-Pei Ch'ao Studies, Rochester, Minnesota, Fall 1977-
Sung Studies, Princeton, 1970-
Ming Studies, Minneapolis, 1975-
Ch'ing-shih wen-t'i 清史問題 St. Louis, 1965-
Chinese Republican Studies Newsletter, Stoors, Connecticut, 1975-
Contemporary China, New York, 1976-

The specialist will therefore be well advised to consult the particular newsletter that concerns his/her field of research, and in case his/her field is not covered, to enquire whether such newsletter has in the meantime been instituted.

K. Geographical Reference Works

Scan the reference works listed in:

1. Yüan Tung-li's *China in Western Literature* [C 2], Chapter IV, "Geography and Travel," pp. 24-54.
2. Teng and Biggerstaff, Chapter IV, "Geographical Works," pp. 156-65.

For older Chinese works on geography see also:

K 1. *Chung-kuo ti-li t'u-chi ts'ung-k'an* 中國地理圖籍叢刊. Wang Yung 王庸. Shanghai: Commercial Press, 1947 (Preface dated 1940). Reprinted Shanghai, 1956.
Despite its comprehensive title, this work deals only with Ming dynasty works. (The Ming dynasty was in fact the first period of comprehensive geographical surveys.)

K 2. *Chung-kuo shu-kang* 中國書綱. Kao Yüeh-t'ien 高越天. Taipei: Wei-hsin, 1971.
The chapter on geographical works (pp. 145-58) lists a number of older works and provides an informative description of the comprehensive surveys (*i-t'ung-chih* 一統志) of Ming and Ch'ing times.

On modern China see:

K 3. *A Geography of China*. Thomas R. Tegear. London: University of London Press, 1965.
A general description of the physical, historical, economic and social geography of the country with a useful bibliography on pp. 325-32.

K 4. *The Geography of China: A Selected and Annotated Bibliography*. Theodore Herman. New York: State Education Dept., 1967. 44 pp.
". . . designed as a guide to important materials and

writings on the geography of China for those who, without previous geographical training, must teach about China at school or university level" (Preface).

GEOGRAPHICAL DICTIONARIES

See Teng and Biggerstaff, pp. 157-8, especially the comments on the two major works:

K 5. *Chung-kuo ku-chin ti-ming ta tz'u-tien* 中國古今地名大辭典. Tsang Li-ho 臧勵龢 and others. Shanghai: Commerical Press, 1931. Repeatedly reprinted, e.g., Taipei, 1960.

K 6. *Chung-kuo ti-ming ta tz'u-tien* 中國地名大辭典. Liu Chün-jen 劉鈞仁. Peking: Kuo-li Pei-p'ing yen-chiu-yüan, 1930. Taipei repr: Wen-hai, 1967.

ROMANIZATION OF PLACE NAMES

For standard romanizations consult the various gazetteers published by the Office of Geography of the U.S. Department of the Interior, e.g.,

K 7. *Mainland China, Administrative Divisions and Their Seats.* Official standard names approved by the U.S. Board on Geographic Names. Washington, D.C.: Office of Geography, 1963.

ATLASES

Read: 1. Berton and Wu Guide, Chapter IV, A "Atlases."
2. Teng and Biggerstaff, Chapter G, 7, "Maps, Atlases and Gazetteers."

Historical Atlases

K 8. *Historical and Commercial Atlas of China.* Albert Herrmann. Cambridge, Mass.: Harvard University Press, 1935. Taipei repr: Ching-wen, 1964.

K 9. *Tōyō dokushi chizu* 東洋讀史地圖 Yanai Watari 箭內互. Tokyo: Fuzambo, 1931.

K 10. *Ajia rekishi chizu* アジア歷史地圖. Matsuda Hisao 松田壽易 and Mori Shikazo 森鹿三. Tokyo: Heibonsha, 1966.
Has Chinese character index by stroke count and a bibliography (p. 14) which also lists Western works of relevance.

K 11. *Chung-kuo li-shih ti-li ta tz'u-tien* 中國歷史地理大辭典. Chang Ch'in 張欽. Chung-hua t'u-shu-kuan, 1913. Taiwan repr: Hsin-wen-shu, 1974, author's name: 章欽.
See Teng and Biggerstaff, p. 149.

Modern Atlases

In addition to those mentioned in Teng and Biggerstaff (pp. 160-2), the following deserve mention here:

K 12. *The Times Atlas of China*. P. J. M. Geelan and D. C. Twitchett, eds. New York: Quadrangle/The New York Times Book Co., 1974.
Read the introduction by the editors.

K 13. *Atlas of China*. Hsieh Chiao-min. New York: McGraw-Hill, 1973.
Maps and tables represent "the principal characteristics of the country, including its physical environment, cultural configuration, regional characteristics and historical evolution." (Preface) Unfavorably reviewed by Jack F. Williams in *JAS* 33.3:471-2 (May 1974), for trying to cover too much, but still a good first geographical reference on modern China.

K 14. *Kung-fei ch'ieh-chü hsia ti Chung-kuo ta-lu fen-sheng ti-t'u* 共匪竊據下的中國大陸分省地圖. Yeh Hsiang-chih 葉翔之. Originally published in the PRC in 1964 for "internal use," this work was reprinted on Taiwan by the College of Chinese Culture in 1966 under the title above.

The best detailed Chinese provincial map atlas available at this time. Descriptive text on verso of maps; 146 pages of ancillary material (參考資料).

Several useful administrative and geographic maps of China have been produced and freely distributed by the U.S. Central Intelligence Agency. Standard English transcriptions of administrative units and place names are used. For reference to detail maps see also:

K 15. *China: an Index to European Visual and Aural Materials.* K. L. Pratt and D. W. S. Gray. London: Crosby Lockwood Staples, 1973; Hamden, Conn.: Shoe String Press, 1973. Pp. 27-36: "Maps."

GAZETTEERS

The Chinese gazetteers (*fang-chih* 方志) or local gazetteers (*ti-fang chih* 地方志) constitute a body of Chinese geographical reference works compiled according to a fairly standardized pattern by local authorities or under their auspices. They are unique primary sources for research into many aspects of local affairs and are therefore receiving increasing attention not only from geographers but also from historians, economists, sociologists, etc. The most comprehensive work on the gazetteers is:

K 16. *Catalogues of Chinese Local Gazetteers.* Donald Daniel Leslie and Jeremy Davidson. Canberra: Australian National University, 1967.
Read the Introduction, pp. xi-xxxii.

Other suggested readings:

K 17. "Local Gazetteers." D. D. Leslie, in *Essays on the Sources for Chinese History* [J 2], pp. 71-82.
This is a shorter, concise description of the gazetteers, with a 12-item bibliography of works written between 1958 to 1969.

K 18. *Fang-chih hsin-lun* 方志新論. Mao I-po 毛一波. Taipei: Cheng-chung, 1974.

K 19. *Chung-kuo ku fang-chih k'ao* 中國古方志考. Chang Kuo-kan 張國淦. Peking: Chung-hua, 1962. Taiwan repr: Ting-wen, 1974.

K 20. *Fang-chih hsüeh* 方志學. Li T'ai-fen 李泰棻. Shanghai: Commercial Press, 1935. Reprinted Taipei, 1968.

Over the years, several union lists of gazetteers and lists of holdings of individual libraries have been published, such as:

K 21. *Chung-kuo ti-fang-chih tsung-lu* 中國地方志綜錄, Chu Shih-chia 朱士嘉. Rev. ed. Shanghai: Commercial Press, 1958

K 22. *Nihon shuyō toshokan kenkyūjo shozō Chūgoku chihō shi sōgō mokuroku* 日本主要圖書館研究所所藏中國地方志總合目錄. Tokyo: National Diet Library, 1969.

K 23. *Chūgoku chihōshi rengō mokuroku* 中國地方志連合目錄. Tokyo: Tōyō Bunko, 1964.

K 24. *T'ai-wan kung-ts'ang fang-chih lien-ho mu-lu* 台灣公藏方志聯合目錄. Taipei: National Central Library, 1957.

Individual catalogs of holdings have been published by the Library of Congress (1942, with a preface, worth reading, by Arthur W. Hummel), the University of Chicago Library (1969), the Library of the University of Washington, Seattle (1966), Cornell's East Asian Library (1964), the Asia Library of the University of Michigan (1968), and the East Asian Library of the University of Pittsburgh (1969).

Due to the rising interest in gazetteers, Taiwan publishers have been engaged in large-scale reprinting. The following publishers and their reprint series are noteworthy in this context:

Ch'eng-wen 成文. Chung-kuo fang-chih ts'ung-shu 中國方志叢書.

Hsüeh-sheng 學生. Hsin-hsiu fang-chih ts'ung-k'an 新修方志叢書.

Hua-wen 華文. Chung-kuo sheng-chih hui-pien 中國省志彙編.

INDEXES TO GEOGRAPHICAL PERIODICALS

K 25. *Chung-kuo ti-hsüeh lun-wen so-yin* 中國地學論文索引. Wang Yung 王庸 and Mao Nai-an 茅乃安, eds. Peking: National Normal University, 1934-36. Taiwan repr: Ku-t'ing, 1970. 2 vols.
See Teng and Biggerstaff, pp. 78-9.

K 26. *Kuo-nei pao-k'an yu kuan ti-li tzu-liao so-yin* 國內報刊有關地理資料索引. Peking: K'o-hsüeh, 1956.
This indexes 53 periodicals and 30 newspapers, but only for the year 1955.

BIBLIOGRAPHIES FOR SPECIAL AREAS

K 27. *Chung-kuo pien-chiang t'u-chi-lu* 中國邊疆圖籍錄. Teng Yen-lin 鄧衍林. Shanghai: Commercial Press, 1958 (from 1939).

K 28. *Hsin-chiang yen-chiu wen-hsien mu-lu, 1886-1962* 新疆研究文獻目錄. Yüan T'ung-li 袁同禮 and Watanabe Hiroshi 渡邊宏 comp. Tokyo: 1962. (Hsin-chiang yen-chiu ts'ung-k'an, n. 2).
Lists Japanese works on Sinkiang; see Berton and Wu Guide, p. 39.

K 29. *Meng-ku ts'an-k'ao shu-mu* 蒙古參考書目. Chang Hsing-t'ang 張興唐. Taipei: Chung-hua ts'ung-shu wei-yüan-hui, 1958.

K 30. *A Hongkong Union Catalogue: Works Relating to Hongkong in Hongkong Libraries.* H. Anthony Rydings. Hongkong, University of Hongkong, 1976.
Contains 3,152 items in Western languages and 1,054 in Chinese relating to Hongkong from the libraries of nine Hongkong institutions.

L. Chinese Biography

In view of its importance, in particular for historical research, Chinese biography deserves special attention. To gain an overview and a full appreciation of the scope of this field, the following reading is suggested:

L 1. Teng and Biggerstaff, pp. 166-91.

L 2. Berton and Wu Guide, pp. 160-73.

L 3. Andrew J. Nathan, *Modern China* [C 7], pp. 23-31.

L 4. "Aspects of Traditional Chinese Biography." David S. Nivison. In *JAS* 21:457-63 (August 1962).

L 5. "Chinese Biographical Writings." Denis Twitchett, in *Confucian Personalities*. Ed. by Arthur F. Wright and Denis Twitchett. Stanford University Press: 1962, pp. 24-39.

L 6. "Die Biographie in China." Peter Olbricht, in *Saeculum* 8:224-35 (1957). (In German).

L 7. *Chung-kuo li-shih yen-chiu kung-chü shu hsü lu* 中國歷史研究工具書敍錄. Tseng Ting-ching 曾影靖. Hongkong: Lung-men, 1968. "Jen-wu" (Biographical Works), pp. 246-91.

A distinction may be made between biographical reference works for China in general and a series of works dealing with one particular historical period, generally defined by a dynastic period.

COMPREHENSIVE BIOGRAPHICAL DICTIONARIES

L 8. *Biographical Dictionaries and Related Works*. Robert Slocum. Detroit: Gale Research Co., 1967; suppl. 1970. The China section of this general bibiography comprises 9 pages (pp. 68-76) and lists 88 important biographical reference works.

L 9. *A Chinese Biographical Dictionary*. Herbert A. Giles. London: Quaritch; Shanghai: Kelly & Walsh, 1989. Repr 1.
This is an old classic, and still the most convenient primary reference source, listing 2,579 prominent Chinese from ancient times to late Ch'ing. It has been criticized for inaccuracies and for lacking information on its sources, see:

L 10. "Einige Verbesserungen zu Giles' Chinese Biographical Dictionary." Erich von Zach, in *Asia Major* 3:545f. (1926).

L 11. "A propos du Chinese Biographical Dictionary de Monsieur H. Giles." Paul Pelliot, in *Asia Major* 4:377f. (1927).

L 12. *The Chinese Reader's Manual: A Handbook of Biographical, Historical, Mythological, and General Literary Reference*. William Frederick Mayers. Shanghai: Presbytarian Missionary Press, 1824; 2nd ed. 1939. Repr 1.
An older, but handy biographical dictionary because of its large selection and concise material. Note also the ancillary material in the appendices.

L 13. *Chung-kuo jen-ming ta tz'u-tien* 中國人名大辭典 Fang I 方毅 and others. Shanghai: Commercial Press, 1921, 2nd ed. 1934. Taiwan repr: Commercial Press, 1977.
The most important Chinese work of this nature; see Teng and Biggerstaff, pp. 166-7. The latest Taiwan edition has a supplement 續編 of 139 pages for the period 1911-1976 with a separate 4-corner index.

L 14. *Chung-kuo wen-hsüeh-chia ta tz'u-tien* 中國文學家大辭典. T'an Cheng-pi 譚正璧. Shanghai: Kuang-ming, 1934. Reprinted on Taiwan and in Hongkong. Taipei repr: Shih-chieh, 1967, author's name: 譚嘉定.
The title is somewhat misleading and should be interpreted loosely, as the work is not strictly a biographical dictionary of "literary personalities." One reason this term was used may be that Chinese political personalities were also literary men.
Read Teng and Biggerstaff, p. 167.

L 15. *Li-tai jen-wu nien-li pei-chuan tsung-piao* 歷代人物年里碑傳總表. Chiang Liang-fu 姜亮夫. Shanghai: Commercial Press, 1937. Reprinted, with somewhat differing titles, in revised and enlarged editions in Peking, 1959; Hongkong, 1961; and Taipei, 1965.

A very important work; read Teng and Biggerstaff, p. 175.

L 16. *Ajia rekishi jiten* アジア歴史事典 . Tokyo: Heibonsha, 1962. 10 vols.

This Japanese encyclopedic dictionary of Asian history contains compact articles on many Chinese historical personalities.

In addition, we recommend the following well-written accounts of certain limited groups of Chinese historical personalities:

L 17. *The Makers of Cathay*. Charles Wilfrid Allan. Shanghai: Presbyterian Mission Press, 1909.

L 18. *China's Leaders in Ideas and Action*. Cornelia Spencer (pseudonym of Grace Yankey Sydenstricker) Philadelphia: Macrae Smith, 1966.

L 19. *The Strain of Harmony: Men and Women in the History of China*. Bernhard Martin. London: W. Heinemann, 1948.

BIOGRAPHICAL REFERENCE WORKS ON PARTICULAR HISTORICAL PERIODS

Much of the material in these works is gleaned from the official dynastic histories. (See pp. 89-91 under "History," where we discuss these official dynastic histories and a biographical index.) Here, we list, in chronological order, material for individual dynasties and periods.

Liao and Chin Dynasties 遼金

L 20. *Ryo Kin Gen jin denki sakuin* 遼金元人傳記索引.

Umehara Kaoru 梅原郁 and Kinugawa Tsuyoshi 衣川強子. Kyōto Daigaku Jimbun Kagaku Kenkyūjo, 1972.

Sung Dynasty 宋

L 21. *Sung-jen chuan-chi tzu-liao so-yin* 宋人傳記資料索引. Ch'ang Pi-te 昌彼得 and others. Taipei: Ting-wen, 1975.

L 22. *Sōjin denki sakuin* 宋人傳記索引. Sōshi Teiyō Hensan Kyōryoku Iinkai. Tokyo: Tōyō Bunko, 1968.

L 23. *Sung Biographies*. Herbert Franke. Wiesbaden, Germany: Steiner, 1976.

Yuan Dynasty 元

See above: *Ryo Kin Gen jin denki sakuin* [L 20].

Ming Dynasty 明

L 24. *An Introduction to the Sources of Ming History.* Wolfgang Franke. Kuala Lumpur: University of Malaya Press, 1968.
Read the introduction (pp. 74-7) to the chapter on biographies.

L 25. *Ming-jen chuan-chi tzu-liao so-yin* 明人傳記資料索引. Taipei: Chung-yang t'u-shu-kuan, 1966. 2 vols.

L 26. *Dictionary of Ming Biography, 1368-1644.* Edited by D. Carrington Goodrich and Chaoying Fang. Ming Biographical History Project of the Association for Asian Studies. New York: Columbia University Press, 1976. 2 vols.
Read review by Willard J. Peterson in *JAS* 38.3:558-61 (May 1979).

Ch'ing Dynasty 清

L 27. *Eminent Chinese of the Ch'ing Dynasty*. Arthur W. Hummel, ed. Washington, D.C.: Govt. Printing Office, 1943 and 1945. 2 vols. Repr 1, in 1 vol.
Although frequently referred to under the editor's name as "the Hummel," most of the contributions are by Fang

Chao-ying 房兆楹 and his wife, Tu Lien-che 杜聯喆. Read the introduction by Hu Shih, dated 1943.

L 28. *Shimmatsu Minsho Chugoku kanshin jimmeiroku* 清末民初中國官紳人名錄. Tahara Jeijiro 田原禎次郎, Peking, 1918. Taiwan repr: Ku-t'ing, 1970.
Note overlap with the Republican era.

L 29. *Ch'ing-tai ch'i-pai ming-jen chuan* 清代七百名人傳. Ts'ai Kuan-lo 蔡冠洛 Shanghai: Shih-chieh, 1937. 3 vols. Reprinted in Hongkong and Taipei. Taipei repr: Ch'i-ming, 1965.

Republican China 民國

In the twenties and thirties, several Who's Whos were published in Shanghai. The general yearbooks for that period are also useful sources of biographical information, as are biographical directories published by the Japanese Ministry of Foreign Affairs. Other important works are:

L 30. *Biographical Dictionary of Republican China*. Howard L. Boorman, ed., Richard C. Howard, assoc. ed. New York: Columbia University Press, 1967-1971. 4 vols.
An extremely valuable work, containing 600 in-depth biographies on the pattern of the "Hummel" [L 27], although it has been criticized for its selection criteria and alleged political bias, see *Book Review Digest* (New York, Wilson Co.) for 1969 and 1972 under the title of the work.

L 31. *Who's Who in Modern China*. Max Perleberg. Hongkong: Ye Old Printerie, 1954.
Data should be used critically, cf. Berton and Wu Guide [C 6], p. 162.

L 32. *Chung-kuo wen-hua-chieh jen-wu tsung-chien* 中國文化界人物總鑑. Hashikawa Tokio 橋川時雄. Peking, 1940. Taiwan repr: Ku-t'ing, 1969.
The scope of this work is 1912-1940.

L 33. *Chung-kuo wen-hua tsung-ho yen-chiu (Chin liu-shih*

nien lai Chung-kuo hsüeh-jen yen-chiu Chung-kuo wen-hua chih kung-hsien) 中國文化綜合研究(近六十年來中國學人研究中國文化之貢獻). Taipei, preface dated 1971.

This work contains 50 biographies of educators and scholars of the past 60 years.

L 34. *Chung-kuo chin-tai jen-wu chuan-chi tzu-liao so-yin* 中國近代人物傳記資料索引. ("Index to Biographical Material on Modern Chinese Personalities"), National Central Library, Taipei, 1973.

Mainly a Taiwan periodical index for the field; see review by Ernst Wolff in *Journal of Library and Information Science* 1.2:151-3 (October 1975).

The Mainland 人民

In the early years of the PRC, it was difficult to obtain biographical data on PRC personalities. The U.S. Consulate General in Hongkong used to publish mimeographed biographical information sheets. Some of Boorman's entries [L 30] overlap into the communist era. Two monographs provide particularly meaningful information and are still recommended for reading:

L 35. *China's Red Masters: Political Biographies of Chinese Communist Leaders*. Robert S. Elegant. New York: Twayne Publishers, 1951.

L 36. *Red Dust*. Helen Snow. Stanford, Calif.: Stanford University Press, 1952.

Subtitle: Autobiographies of Chinese Communists as told to Nym Wales (pseudonym of author).

The most comprehensive work so far, however, is:

L 37. *Biographical Dictionary of Chinese Communism, 1921-1965*. Donald W. Klein and Anne B. Clark, Cambridge: Harvard University Press, 1971.

This dictionary "should long remain an indispensable reference book. . . . It contains 433 biographical sketches, ranging from half a page (Hui Yü-yü) to fifteen (Chou En-lai)." Hsüeh Chün-tu in his review of the book, *JAS* 31. 1:405-7 (February 1972). Note also the many appendixes and the bibliography on pp. 1031-8 which lists practically all sources and previous works.

Supplementary sources:

L 38. *Gendai Chūgoku jimmei jiten* 現代中國人名辭典. Japanese Ministry of Foreign Affairs. Tokyo: Kazankai, 1978.
Scope: up to end of 1977.

L 39. *Directory of Officials of the PRC.* U.S. Central Intelligence Agency, Washington D.C., August 1972.
This agency also occasionally publishes reference aids of biographical nature, e.g., on Central Committee members, provincial party leaders, organizational tables, etc., giving reliable and up-to-date information on data that are subject to constant change.

L 40. *Who's Who in Communist China.* Union Research Institute, Hongkong.
Published at irregular intervals, the latest dated 1969 has its cut-off date 5 September 1968.

L 41. *On Mao Tse-tung, a Bibliographic Guide.* Austin C. W. Shu. Asian Studies Center, Michigan State University, East Lansing, Mich., 1972.

L 42. *The Cultural Revolution in China: An Annotated Bibliography.* James C. F. Wang. New York: Garland, 1976.

L 43. *Chinaköpfe, Kurzbiographien der Partei-und Staatsfunktionäre der Volksrepublic China.* Wolfgang Bartke. Hannover: Verlag für Literatur und Zeitgeschehen, 1966.

L 44. *Chung-kung jen-ming lu* 中共人名錄. Taipei: Research Institute of International Relations, 1978, rev. 1967 ed.

L 45. *Fei-tang chung-yang jen-shih tzu-liao* 匪黨中央人事資料. Chung-kuo kuo-min-tang, Chung-yang wei-yüan-hui, Ti liu tsu. Taipei, 1960.

L 46. *Chung-kung shou-yao shih-liao hui-pien* 中共首要事略彙編. Li Feng-min 李鳳敏. Taipei: Chung-kung yen-chiu tsa-chih she, 1969. Supplement 1972.

L 47. *Chuka jimmin kyōwakoku soshikibetsu jimmei hyō* 中華人民共和國組織別人名表. Japan, Naikaku Kambo, Naikaku Chōsashitsu. Tokyo, 1961.

Taiwan: 台灣

The official *China Yearbook* [Q 4], published annually on Taiwan, has a useful biographical section with short entries. As a possible source of biographical information we may also mention here:

L 48. *Chuan-chi wen-hsüeh* 傳記文學. Taipei: Chuan-chi wen-hsüeh tsa-chih she, 1962-. Monthly.
This is a periodical entirely devoted to autobiographical reminiscences of contemporary personalities. Most of the material is from the Republican era, some extending into the ROC period on Taiwan.

CHINESE NAMES AND KINSHIP DESIGNATIONS

The problem of verifying a Chinese name is frequently encountered in biographical searches and requires some elucidation. The first problem is to distinguish the various forms of a name and to determine the "formal" name. According to our usage it should consist of a surname (family name, *hsing* 姓) and one fixed given name (*ming* 名). In addition, however, there are:

shih	氏	clan or family name (particularly for women)
hsiao-ming	小名	childhood name, also *ju-ming* 孺名 or *nai-ming* 奶名
tzu	字	style, courtesy name used by a person's friends (usually given by his family)

hao	號	fancy name (usually given by friends)
pieh-hao	別號	studio name, poetic name (chosen by person himself/herself)
pi-ming	筆名	pseudonym of writers, nom-de-plume
wai	外號	nickname, also *cho-hao* 綽號 *hun-hao* 混號 *hun-hao* 諢號
nien-hao	年號	reign name of emperors (see p. 91).
shih	謚	posthumous name of emperor or high official
hui	諱	taboo name, personal name of respected person, such as emperor, father (see p. 92)

Although some sources list as many as 4,000 Chinese surnames, the number of common surnames is only somewhat above 200. A listing of surnames by an anonymous compiler of the Sung dynasty is:

L 49. *Pai chia hsing* 百家姓 .
Used as a primer to teach elementary school children the surnames, of which it lists 406 single-character and 30 double-character names. Apart from starting with the imperial family name *chao* 趙 there is no apparent order in this listing.

L 50. "The Family Names." Herbert Giles in *NCBRAS* 21:255-88 (1886).
An alphabetical arrangement of the *Po-chia-hsing* with genealogical notes.

Suggested readings on the *Pai-chia-hsing:*

L 51. "Genealogy and origin of Chinese family names." Kiang Kang-hu in *Il Marco Polo* 4.15:21-9 (1943).

L 52. "Po-chia-hsing." I-shih 一士, in *Hsing-ming chang-ku* 姓名掌故. Hongkong: Chung-shan, 1974, p. 1.

There are no limitations on parental inventiveness as to personal names in China, but in actual practice certain characters are preferred for superstitious and esthetic reasons, or the customary use of *meng, chung, chi* 孟仲季 or *po, chung, shu, chi* 伯仲叔季 for oldest, second, third and youngest sons. In most families a generation order is expressed by one common character in the personal names of the same generation, the so-called *p'ai-hang* 排行 order.

Suggested readings:

L 53. *Der chinesische Personenname*. Wolfgang Bauer. Wiesbaden: Harrassowitz, 1959.
Non-German readers may find the copious bibliography on pp. 390-406 of great usefulness.

L 54. *Chung-kuo jen-ming ti yen-chiu* 中國人名的研究. Hsiao Yao-t'ien 蕭遙天. Penang: Chiao-yü ch'u-pan kung-ssu, 1970.

L 55. *China*. Nagel Publishers. English version by Anne L. Desteney. Geneva: Nagel, 1973. See pp. 326-31.

L 56. "Chung-kuo-jen hsing-ming ti lai-li" 中國人姓名的來歷. Li Chia-fu 李甲孚, in *Tsu-kuo i-chou* 祖國一週 355:13-6 (23 April 1972).

Studio Names and Pseudonyms

There are two important reference tools for these names:

L 57. *Ku-chin jen-wu pieh-ming so-yin* 古今人物別名索引. Ch'en Te-yün 陳德芸. Canton: Lingnan University Library, 1937. Taiwan repr: Yi-wen, 1965.
Read description and evaluation in Teng and Biggerstaff, p. 188.

L 58. *Shih-ming pieh-hao so-yin* 室名別號索引. Ch'en Nai-ch'ien 陳乃乾. Peking: Chung-hua, 1957. Reprinted in Hongkong and Taipei.
Read description in Teng and Biggerstaff, p. 189.

There is a long list of other works on pseudonyms of which the following deserve mention:

L 59. *Twentieth Century Chinese Writers and Their Pen Names.* Chu Pao-liang. Boston: C. K. Hall, 1977. 364pp. Read review by Nelson Chou in *J of Chinese Language Teachers Assoc.* 4.2: 103-7 (May 1979).

L 60. *Modern Chinese Authors, a List of Pseudonyms.* Austin Chi-wei Shu 舒紀維. 2nd rev. ed. Taipei: Chinese Materials and Research Aids Service Center, 1971. Read the Introduction.

L 61. *Pi-ming yin-te* 筆名引得. Chang T'ai-ku 張泰谷. Taipei: Wen-hai, 1971.
See the introduction, which refers to 2 related lists.

L 62. "Min-kuo tso-chia pi-ming lu" 民國作家筆名錄. Ch'in Hsien-tz'u 秦賢次, in *Hsin-chih tsa-chih* 新知雜誌(Taipei) 4.1, 2, 3, 5 (1974).
Has a bibliography on the subject of pseudonyms.

L 63. "Pi-ming pieh-hao chien-tzu piao" 筆名別號檢字表. Yü Ping-kuen 余秉權, in *Chung-kuo shih-hsüeh lun-wen yin-te hsü-pien* 中國史學論文引得續編. Cambridge, Mass.: Harvard-Yending Library, 1970, pp. 19-24.

L 64. *Hsin-hai i-hou shih-ch'i nien chih-kuan piao,* See [J 102] Lists alternative names for officials during 1912-1928 period.

L 65. "Tso-chia pi-ming i lan" 作家筆名一覽. Wang Che-fu 王哲甫, in *Chung-kuo hsin wen-hsüeh yün-tung shih* 中國新文學運動史, Peking: Ching-shan, 1933.
Hongkong repr: Yüan-tung, 1965.

L 66. *An Index to the Biographical Notices of Authors in the Ch'u-pan chou-k'an* (出版週刊). Lienche Fang, comp. Berkeley, 1958. Mimeographed.
Read the introduction.

L 67. *Ch'ing-tai shu hua chia tzu-hao yin-te* 清代書畫家字號引得. ("Index to the Fancy Names of the Calligraphers and Painters of the Ch'ing Dynasty"). Ts'ai Chin-chung 蔡金重 Peking: Harvard-Yenching Institute, 1932. (Harvard-Yenching Institute Sinological Index no. 21) Taipei repr: Ch'eng-wen 1966.

L 68. "Hsing-ming pieh-hao 姓名別號" Tseng Ying-ching, see [J 5] pp. 285-91.

Kinship Terms

Chinese kinship terms are more elaborate and specific than those in Western languages. Information on these terms may be obtained from the following sources:

L 69. "The Chinese kinship system." Feng Han-yi, in *HJAS* 2.2:141-275 (July 1937).
This article was reprinted as No. 22 (1967) of the Harvard-Yenching Institute Studies series.

L 70. "Chinese family nomenclature." H. P. Wilkinson, in *New China Review* 3.3:159-91 (June 1921).

L 71. "Chinese terms of address." Chao Yuen-ren in *Language* 32.1:217-41 (Jan.-March 1956).
Note the useful bibliography in footnote 1.

Further references may be found in the Skinner bibliography [C 9] in the chapter "Kin Terms and Relationships." The Catholic Mission at Hsienhsien also published a table:

L 72. "La Famille Wang, un tableau de la parenté chinoise." Etienne Merveille and J. M. De Kermadec. Hsien-hsien, n.d.
The table shows the position in the family tree of its various members and the Chinese designations of these various positions.

Japanese Names

The frequent occurrence, in connection with China studies, of Japanese names written in Chinese characters makes it necessary to provide guides for the correct reading of such names.

Suggested introductory reading:

L 73. *ZH Guide* by G. Kennedy [E 50] pp. 63-71.

L 74. *Research in Japanese Sources, a Research Guide*. Herschel Webb with the assistance of Marleigh Ryan. New York: Columbia University Press, 1965.
Read, in particular, p. 51.

Actual name lists giving alphabetical transcriptions are:

L 75. *Japanese Surnames*. I. V. Gillis and Pai Ping-ch'i. Peking: Hwa Hsing Press, 1939.

L 76. *Japanese Personal Names*. I. V. Gillis and Pai Ping-ch'i. Peking: Hwa Hsing Press, 1940.

L 77. *Japanese Names*. P. G. O'Neill. New York: John Weatherhill, 1972.
Note the bibliography of related works on p. viii.

L 78. *Modern Japanese Authors in Area Studies: A Namelist*. Austin C. W. Shu. San Francisco: Chinese Materials Center, 1978.
A convenient listing for China scholars of several thousand 20th century Japanese scholars, also listed according to their area specialization.

With a knowledge of Japanese *kana* a more "professional" approach would be to refer to one of the Japanese works, such as:

L 79. *Nanori jiten* 名乘辭典. Araki Ryōzō 荒木良造. Tokyo: Tōkyodō, 1964.

L 80. *Dai jimmei jiten* 大人名事典. Tokyo: Heibonsha, 1953-55. 10 vols.

L 81. *Chosakuken daichō* 著作權台帳 ("Copyright Register"). Tokyo, Nippon Chosakuken Kyōgikai. Published annually. Difficult to use but indispensible for locating the pronunciation of modern writers' names.

L 82. *Jitsuyō nandoku kisei jiten* 實用難讀奇姓辭典. Shinozaki Teruo 篠崎晃雄. Tokyo: Nippon Kajo Shuppan Sha, 1973.

L 83. *Jitsuyō seishi jiten* 實用姓氏辭典. Tokyo: Kabushiki Kaisha Meringu, 1966.

Nien-p'u 年譜

The *nien-p'u* is a unique Chinese form of biography which is frequently encountered. It is sometimes autobiographical (*tzu-ting nien-p'u* 自定年譜) as in the case of K'ang Yu-wei's. In its most common, almost standardized, form it lists a person's life data and literary achievements in chronological order and gives excerpts from his writings. In some cases it gives information on other persons mentioned and certain details about their lives. *Nien-p'u* are frequently attached to the collection of a person's literary works, some are found in *ts'ung-shu* 叢書 (see section I).

References for further study:

L 84. "Nien-p'u k'ao-lüeh" 年譜考略. Liang T'ing-ts'an 梁廷燦, in *Kuo-li Pei-p'ing T'u-shu-kuan kuan-k'an* 3.1-5 (1929).

L 85. *Chung-kuo li-tai ming-jen nien-p'u mu-lu* 中國歷代名人年譜目錄. Li Shih-t'ao 李士濤. Shanghai: Commercial Press, 1941.
Described in Teng and Biggerstaff, p. 177; lists 1,108 biographies of 964 persons, with a 4 corner index.

L 86. "Das Niän-pu: Eine Untersuchung zu den literarischen Formen chinesischer Biographien." Luise Stoll. Darmstadt: Wittich, 1935.
Ph.D. dissertation at the University of Frankfurt a.M., Germany, dated 31 May 1935.

M. Philosophy and Religion

Confucianism, Buddhism and Taoism are often referred to as the three major religions of China. Apart from the question whether Confucianism is in fact a religion, this grouping omits Islam, Christianity, and Judaism, each of which has had a noteworthy influence in Chinese history. The wide field of Chinese mythology overlaps that of religion and is inseparably linked with it. Philosophy is also often difficult to separate from religion in China, especially in premodern times. The bibliographic aids to all these fields will therefore be treated together, if in a limited and highly selective fashion.

PHILOSOPHY IN GENERAL

The volume of writings on Chinese philosophy is immense. For the Western reader, the following are suggested basic works:

M 1. *An Outline and an Annotated Bibliography of Chinese Philosophy*. Wing-tsit Chan 陳榮捷. New Haven: Far Eastern Publications, Yale University, 1961.
An outstanding work and so far the most comprehensive bibliography of the field.

M 2. *A Source Book of Chinese Philosophy*. Wing-tsit Chan. Princeton, N. J.: Princeton University Press, 1963.
Mainly provides translated and annotated excerpts. This book also contains a substantial bibliography on pp. 793-811.

M 3. *A History of Chinese Philosophy*. Fung Yu-lan 馮友蘭. Translated by Derk Bodde. Princeton, N.J.: Princeton University Press, 1952-53. 2 vols.

M 4. *A Short History of Chinese Philosophy*. Fung Yu-lan. Edited by Derk Bodde. New York: Macmillan, 1960.
Meant to be "suggestive rather than exhaustive," this book contains a solid bibliography on pp. 343-50.

On the subject of Chinese philosophy under the impact of Western ideas see in particular:

M 5. *Fifty Years of Chinese Philosophy, 1898-1948.* O. Brière. Translated by Laurence G. Thompson. London: Allen and Unwin, 1956.
Includes a rich bibliography for the period under review, see pp. 111-48.

M 6. *Scientism in Chinese Thought 1900-1950.* D. W. Y. Kwok. New Haven: Yale University Press, 1965.
Note bibliography, pp. 205-23.

On philosophy in mainland China see:

M 7. *Chinese Philosophy, 1949-1963: An Annotated Bibliography of Mainland China Publications.* Wing-tsit Chan. Honolulu: East-West Center Press, 1967.

M 8. *Chinese Studies in Philosophy* (A Journal of Translations). White Plains, N.Y.: Sharpe, 1969-
A quarterly journal featuring mainland Chinese articles in English translation.

Major periodicals covering the entire field of Chinese philosophy:

M 9. *Philosophy East and West.* Honolulu: East-West Center Press, 1951- Quarterly.

M 10. *Journal of Chinese Philosophy.* Dordrecht, Holland and Boston, Mass.: Reidel, 1973-
A quarterly "devoted to the study of Chinese philosophy and Chinese thought in all their phases and stages of articulation and development."

RELIGION IN GENERAL

While the topic of Chinese religion is also an immense subject and would appear to call for a commensurate bibliographic treatment, I am fortunately able to limit this coverage to short paragraphs—shortest, paradoxical as it may seem, in the most important branches of Confucianism and Buddhism—because of the excellent coverage these subjects have received in the following bibliography:

M 11. *Studies of Chinese Religion: A Comprehensive and Classified Bibliography of Publications in English, French and German Through 1970.* Laurence G. Thompson, comp., with the assistance of Justine Pinto. Enrico, Calif.: Dickenson, 1976.
This bibliography is comprehensive, indeed, in regard to the subjects treated, but certain relevant areas are excluded: see preface, pp. vii-viii, where Thompson specifically asserts that "it is as possible and necessary to distinguish religion from philosophy in the case of China as in the case of the West." Note the detailed table of contents of this work and scan the chapter "Bibliography and General Studies" (pp. 1-10).

On more recent developments in the People's Republic, the Thompson bibliography lists fifty-eight entries in chapter 37, "Religion under Communism," the most important of which is:

M 12. *Religion in Communist China.* Richard C. Bush. Nashville: Abington Press, 1970.
Further bibliographic references on this topic are to be found in the footnotes of this monograph, which has also chapters entitled "Islam," "Buddhism," "Confucius and His Changing Fortunes," "Taoism," and "Folk Religion: Elusive as Always."

CHINESE MYTHOLOGY

Mythology is a broad field, overlapping that of religion, and including folklore and popular customs. The Thompson bibliography [M 11] provides a substantial list of the main works, altogether 73 entries in chapter 3, "Mythology," of which the following deserve special mention:

M 13. *A Dictionary of Chinese Mythology*. E. T. C. Werner. Shanghai: Kelly and Walsh, 1932. Repr 2.
Although old, this work is still useful for quick primary information.

M 14. "Chinese Mythology." John C. Ferguson, in *The Mythology of All Races*, vol 8., edited by John A. MacCulloch. Boston: Marshall Jones, 1937.
Comparable to *A Dictionary of Chinese Mythology*, but in narrative form and illustrated.

M 15. *Chinese Mythology*. Anthony Christie. Feltham, Middlesex: Hamlyn, 1968.
A more scholarly treatment of the field than the *Dictionary of Chinese Mythology*. "Further reading list" on p. 136.

CONFUCIANISM

Whether considered a religion or not, Confucianism has been for centuries the ruling ideology of the Chinese elite and the spiritual and ethical guide of the Chinese people. See the Thompson bibliography, chapter 7, "Confucius and Confucianism," chapter 8, "Ethics and Morals," and chapter 9 "Filial Piety." For more detailed study we particularly recommend:

M 16. *Confucius, the Man and the Myth*. Herlee G. Creel. New York: J. Day Co., 1949.

M 17. *A Short History of Confucian Philosophy*. Liu Wu-chi. New York: Dell, 1955.
Contains a selected bibliography of English and Chinese books on pp. 207-17.

BUDDHISM

A classic treatment of the history of Chinese Buddhism is:

M 18. *Buddhism in China: A Historical Survey*. Kenneth K. S. Ch'en. Princeton, N. J.: Princeton University Press, 1964. This comprehensive work also contains a bibliography on pp. 505-48.

In the Thompson bibliography [M 11], Part 3 is devoted to Chinese Buddhism.

One of the great problems in dealing with Buddhism is terminology, mostly imported Indian terms, hence the need for good dictionaries. The two most useful from the English-speaker's point of view are:

M 19. *A Dictionary of Chinese Buddhist Terms with Sanskrit and English Equivalents and a Sanskri-Pali Index*. William E. Soothill and Lewis Hodous. London: Kegan Paul, 1937. Repr 1.

M 20. *Japanese-English Buddhist Dictionary*. Tokyo: Daitō Shuppansha, 1965.
Includes index of Chinese characters by stroke count and of romanized Chinese names and Sanskrit-Pali terms arranged alphabetically.

There is a large array of Chinese and Japanese dictionaries, in particular:

M 21. *Fo-hsüeh ta tz'u-tien* 佛學大辭典 Ting Fu-pao 丁福保. Originally published Shanghai, 1925. Taipei reprint: San-hui hsüeh-she, 1974.
See Teng and Biggerstaff, pp. 150-1.

M 22. *Bukkyo daijiten* 佛教大辭典. Mochizuki Shinkō 望月信亨, Tokyo: Sekai Seiten Kankō Kyōkai, 1960-1963. 10 vols. (Originally published 1909-1936.)

Also noteworthy is the following periodical index produced on Taiwan:

M 23. *Chung-hua min-kuo liu-shih nien lai Fo-chiao lun-wen mu-lu* 中華民國六十年來佛教論文目錄. Taipei: Chinese Buddhist Society, 1975.

TAOISM

Taoism evolved from the early philosophical school of Lao-tzu and Chuang-tzu into a philosophical and religious movement of many facets mainly emphasizing individuality, spontaneity, and naturalness, in conscious contrast and rivalry with Confucianism. The reader is referred to the Thompson bibliography which deals in great detail with Taoism on pp. 46-61.

An additional reading we suggest:

M 24. *Le Taoism.* Nicole Vandier-Nicolas. Paris: Presses Universitaires de France, 1965.
A concise (126 pp.) well-written introduction, in which the non-French reader will find the selective bibliography on pp. 127-31 a useful reference tool.

On relevant Chinese reference works, see Teng and Biggerstaff under "Taoism and Buddhism," pp. 38-9.

ISLAM

Islam was brought to China by Persian, Arabian, and Turkish traders, both overland through Central Asia and by sea via India, as early as T'ang and Sung times. As the Chinese empire expanded, it acquired a large Muslim population, especially in the border regions.

Suggested readings:

M 25. *Islam in China: A Neglected Problem.* Marhsall Broomhall. London: Morgan and Scott, 1910.
Still considered the basic work on the history of Islam in China. Note bibliography on pp. 307-10.

M 26. *Chugoku ni okeru Kaikyō no denrai to sono guzū* 中國における回教の傳來とその弘通. Tazaka Kōdō 田坂興道. Tokyo: Toyo Bunko, 1964. 2 vols.
The table of contents is also in English. Note the substantial bibliography on pp. 1688-1726.

A useful reference tool is:

M 27. *Annotated Bibliography of Literature on Islam in China.* Claude L. Pickens. Hankow: Society of Friends of the Moslems in China, 1950.
Originally an MA Thesis at Columbia University, 1945.

For Chinese works on the subject see:

M 28. *Chung-kuo Hui-chiao shih* 中國回教史. Fu T'ung-hsien 傅統先. Taipei: Commercial Press, 1069. Tokyo reprint: Hara Shobo, 1975.
Bibliography on pp. 280-283.

M 29. *Hui-chiao kai-lun* 回教概論. ("An introduction to the Islamism") Hsieh Sung-t'ao 謝松濤. Yang-ming-shan, Taiwan: Hua-kuang, 1976.
Bibliography on pp. 117-18.

CHRISTIANITY

The first historical contact of China with Christianity was as the religion of an ethnic minority, the Nestorian Christians who reached China in the 7th century. Serious missionary activity started with the Jesuits; Mateo Ricci came to Peking in 1601. After three centuries of Catholic and Protestant missionary activity, the number of Chinese Christians still remains comparatively small, although the indirect influence of Christianity on the course of modernization in China has been considerable. For a substantial bibliography see the chapter "Christianity and Foreign Missions" in Yüan Tung-li's *China in Western Literature* [C 2], pp. 326-69, also "Christian

Missions and Their Impact to 1900" (Bibliographical Essay) in the *Cambridge History of China*, vol. 10, [J 3], pp. 611-4.

Suggested further reading:

M 30. *A History of Christian Missions in China*. K. S. Latourette. New York: Macmillan, 1929.

M 31. "China." J. Krahl, in *New Catholic Encyclopedia*. Washington, D.C.: Catholic University of America, 1967, vol. 3, pp. 591-602.
A concise, informative article with a well-selected bibliography on pp. 601-2.

M 32. *A Bibliography of the History of Christianity in China* (A Preliminary Draft). Jonathan T'ien-en Chao 趙天恩. Faculty-in-Preparation, China Graduate School of Theology, Waltham, Mass., 1970.
Based on the holdings of the Missionary Research Library, New York, Harvard-Yenching Library, and University of Pennsylvania Library.

JUDAISM

Although Judaism has never been a "Chinese religion," the existence of Jewish communities in ancient China, especially in Kaifeng, has attracted attention as an interesting historical phenomenon. Only in fairly recent times have these colonies been completely sinicized and lost their separate identity.

Suggested readings:

M 33. *Chinese Jews*. William Charles White. 2nd ed. with additional material and an introduction by Cecil Roth. University of Toronto Press, 1966.
White had been Anglican bishop in Kaifeng for 25 years and originally published his research on the Jews in a 3-volume work in 1942. The second edition prepared and introduced by Cecil Roth adds some material and sup-

plements the bibliography which now appears on p. 16 of the introduction and on pp. 205-6 of Part I.

M 34. *The Survival of the Chinese Jews: The Jewish Community of Kaifeng.* Donald Daniel Leslie. Leiden: Brill, 1972. A "final summing up" and the "first real synthesis" of all known sources on the Kaifeng Jews. Read the introduction and scan "Bibliography and References" on pp. 225-37.

Some of the older, out-of-print material on the Chinese Jews is being collected and republished by Paragon Book Reprint Corp., New York, edited and introduced by Hyman Kublin, under such titles as *Studies of the Chinese Jews: Selected Articles from Journals East and West* (1971), *Jews in Old China: Some Western Views* (1971). *The Orphan Colony of Jews in China* by James Finn, originally London 1872, was reprinted by Ch'eng-wen, Taipei, 1971.

N. Art and Archeology

This is an immense field, as can be expected in a culture four to five thousand years old. I cite only a few general guides and such bibliographies—where they exist—as focus on particular Chinese specialties. There is a large number of books providing general surveys or introductions to Chinese art, such as, for example:

N 1. *The Romance of Chinese Art*. Encyclopaedia Britannica. Garden City, N.Y.: Garden City Publishing Company, 1936.
Reproduces texts and illustrations from the 14th edition of the Encyclopaedia Britannica on 16 Chinese art forms, written by experts in each field, with bibliographies (pp. 189-92). Later editions of the encyclopaedia follow this pattern and can be recommended as starting points for individual studies.

N 2. *The T. L. Yuan Bibliography of Western Writings on Chinese Art and Archaeology*. Harrie A. Vanderstappen, ed. London: Mansell, 1975.
A truly comprehensive bibliography of Western writings on Chinese art and archeology. Initiated by Yüan T'ung-li, but published after his death, it lists over 15,000 items published between 1920 and 1965, classified by subject with detailed subdivisions and an alphabetical author index. Read The Foreword by T. H. Tsien and The Introduction by Vanderstappen, and scan The Table of Contents, pp. xxxvii-xlvii. A welcome feature of this bibliography is that it cites reviews of individual titles.

N 3. *Premodern China: A Bibliographic Introduction*. Chang Chun-shu. Ann Arbor, Michigan: University of Michigan, Center for Chinese Studies, 1971.
Lists Western language materials only. See chapter 4,

"Ancient China in Legendary Traditions," Chapter 5, "Prehistory, Archaeological Findings and Methodology," and "Archaeology and the Arts" under each historical period.

As guides to the special terminology met with in Chinese art and archeology, the following reference works are recommended:

N 4. *A Glossary of Chinese Art and Archaeology*. S. Howard Hansford. London: China Society, 2nd revised edition, 1961.
Noteworthy in the revised edition are the drawings of ritual bronzes, decorative patterns, etc., with a guide to terminology, pp. 88-96.

N 5. *Some Technical Terms of Chinese Paintings*. Benjamin March. Baltimore: Waverly Press, 1935.

PAINTING AND CALLIGRAPHY

Apart from the technical terms (see above) a particular problem in Chinese painting and calligraphy is the identification of names and seals used by the artists. In addition to the reference works mentioned in the T. L. Yuan bibliography [N 2], there are:

N 6. *Chin T'ang i-lai shu-hua-chia chien-ts'ang-chia k'uan-yin p'u* 晉唐以來書畫家鑑藏家款印譜. ("Signatures and Seals of Artists, Connoisseurs and Collectors on Painting and Calligraphy since Tsin Dynasty"). Joint Board of National Palace Museum and National Central Museum, Taichung, Taiwan, 1964. 6 vols.
"This book is published particularly for foreigners," says the English preface. Vol. 4 gives brief biographies of artists.

N 7. *Chung-kuo ming-hua-chia ts'ung-shu* 中國名畫家叢書. (A Collection on Famous Painters in Chinese History), Hongkong: Chung-kuo shu-hua yen-chiu hui, 1970. 2 vols.

Contains biographies of painters and copious black-and-white reproductions. The text is in simplified characters which would indicate that this is the reproduction (without bibliographical data) of an earlier mainland publication.

PERFORMING AND VISUAL ARTS/MUSIC

These are topics frequently not included in reference books on Chinese art. For an introduction into the subject and bibliography see:

N 8. "The Performing and Visual Arts and Music." Richard Fu-sen Yang, in Wu Yüan-li's *China Handbook* [C 15], pp. 737-758.
Some of the subjects included are "The Chinese Opera," "The Modern Drama (hua-chü)," "Motion Pictures," and "Music, Musicals and Ballet."

N 9. *An Annotated Bibliography of Materials for the Study of the Peking Opera*. Daniel S. P. Yang. Madison: University of Wisconsin Press, 1967.

N 10. *Chinese Music, an Annotated Bibliography*. Frederic Lieberman. New York: Garland Publ., Inc., 2nd revised and enlarged edition, 1979.
"Exhaustive coverage of publications in Western languages as well as critical annotations on Chinese music, dance, and drama." (Preface)

N 11. *Chung-kuo hsi-chü t'u-shu mu-lu* 中國戲劇圖書目錄. Hongkong: Chinese University, United College Library. 2 vols, 1967 and 1970.
Lists the substantial holdings of this library in the fields of Chinese modern plays (*hua-chü*) and translations into Chinese of foreign works.

ARCHEOLOGY

This topic is adequately dealt with in T. L. Yüan's bibliography [N 2], in particular in the chapter on "Archaeology," pp. 47-54 and 244-66. For a short introduction (in German) and a succinct 9-item bibliography see also:

N 12. "Archäologie." Magdalene von Dewall, in W. Franke's *China-Handbuch* [C 17], pp. 42-3.

To keep up with the very active pursuit of excavations on the mainland, two journals are essential:

N 13. *Early China* (formerly "Pre-Han China"). Berkeley, California: Society for the Study of Early China, 1975-

N 14. *K'ao-ku* 考古 (formerly *K'ao-ku t'ung-hsün* 考古通訊). Peking: K'ao-ku tsa-chih she, 1955-

O. Dissertations on China

Dissertations are usually the result of very intensive research efforts on a particular, well-defined subject. Even in the case of mediocre or inadequate scholarship, they usually have very extensive bibliographies on a particular subject and may therefore be valuable reference sources.

In the past, there have been many bibliographic compilations of dissertations. Yüan T'ung-li 袁同禮 (1895-1965), one of the pioneers of modern librarianship in China, compiled three bibliographies of dissertations by Chinese students abroad (they frequently chose topics related to China), namely:

O 1. *A Guide to Doctoral Dissertations by Chinese Students in America, 1905-1960*. Washington, D.C.: Sino-American Cultural Society, 1961.

O 2. "Doctoral Dissertations by Chinese Students in Great Britain and Northern Ireland, 1916-1961." *Chinese Culture* 4.4:107-37 (March 1963).

O 3. "A guide to doctoral dissertations by Chinese Students in Continental Europe, 1907-1962." *Chinese Culture* 5.3:98-156 (March 1964); 5.4:81-149 (June 1964); 6.1:79-98 (October 1964).

For a discussion of the three items above see Berton and Wu Guide, Nos. 1883-1885.

For American dissertations on China see:

O 4. *American Doctoral Dissertations on Asia, 1933-1962*. Curtis W. Stucki. Ithaca, N.Y.: Cornell University Press, 1963.

Covering the period of great expansion of China studies in the United States and in Europe, is:

O 5. *Doctoral Dissertations on China: A Bibliography of Stud-*

ies in Western Languages, 1945-1970. Leonard H. D. Gordon and Frank J. Shulman. Seattle: University of Washington Press, 1972.

Note in particular the bibliography on pp. 207-10. Reviewed by G. Raymond Nunn in *JAS* 32:126-29 (1972).

O 6. *Doctoral Dissertations on China, 1971-1975: A Bibliography of Studies in Western Languages*. Frank J. Shulman. Seattle: University of Washington Press, 1978.

It has the added feature of indicating when and if the dissertation was published in book form. A new volume, covering 1976-1980, has been promised for 1982.

P. Newspapers and Periodicals

The history of newspapers and periodicals in China began with the Jesuits who published *Memoires concernant les . . . chinois* (annual from 1776) and later the *Lettres édifiantes et curieuses*, with a German edition, *Welt-Bote*. The Protestant missionaries (Morrison and Milne) started periodicals in Malacca, later Hongkong and Shanghai. In the latter two places the Chinese learned the methods of newspaper publication and later started their own newspapers.

Suggested reading:

P 1. "Jesuit sources." Paul A. Rule, in *Essays on the Sources of Chinese History* [J 2], pp. 176-87.

P 2. "Chinese newspapers." Josef Fass, in *Essays on the Sources of Chinese History* [J 2], pp. 221-8.

P 3. *The Chinese Periodical Press, 1800-1912*. Roswell S. Britton. Shanghai: Kelly and Walsh, 1933. Repr 1.

P 4. *A History of the Press and Public Opinion in China*. Lin Yutang. Shanghai: Kelly and Walsh, 1936.

P 5. *Chung-kuo pao-hsüeh shih* 中國報學史. Ko Kung-chen 戈公振. Shanghai: Commercial Press, 1927. Peking reprinted, 1955; Taipei: Hsüeh-sheng, 1964.

P 6. *Chung-kuo hsin-wen shih* 中國新聞史. Tseng Hsü-pai, ed. 曾虛白. Mu-cha (Taiwan): Cheng-chih ta-hsüeh, 1966. 2 vols. Bibliography on pp. 967-77.

Also read the introductions to the sections on newspapers and periodicals in the Berton and Wu Guide [C 6], pp. 88-104, and in A. J. Nathan's *Modern China* [C 7], pp. 33-8 and 43-7; pp. 40-2 of the latter work deal with Red Guard publications during the Cultural Revolution.

P 7. *Chinese Periodicals: A Guide to Indexes and Periodicals relating to China*. May Ts'ao. New Haven: Mimeographed, 1965.

P 8. *Research Materials on 20th Century China*. P. K. Yu. Washington, D.C.: Center for Chinese Research Materials, 1975.
See in particular pp. 1-86 and pp. 271-3 on Red Guard material published during the Cultural Revolution.

There are many union lists and library holding lists of Chinese periodicals in China and in other countries. Some of the important ones are:

P 9. *Ch'üan-kuo chung-wen ch'i-k'an lien-ho mu-lu* 全國中文期刊聯合目錄. Peking: Pei-ching t'u-shu-kuan, 1961.
This Chinese union list lists 19,115 titles of "scholarly value," even though some were published under "the reactionary regime of the past" (see preface). The scope is from 1833 to 1949 and for this period it is an indispensable reference tool for the identification of Chinese periodicals.

P 10. *Chung-wen ch'i-k'an mu-lu 1949-1956* 中文期刊目錄. Shanghai: Shang-hai shih pao-k'an-t'u-shu-kuan, 1956-1957. 2 vols.
As the scope is 1881-1956, it can be used partially to update the preceding list. No more recent lists are yet available.

P 11. *Union Card File of Oriental Vernacular Serials (Chinese, Japanese, Korean).*
This union file is being maintained at the Orientalia Division of the Library of Congress. A microfilm copy (1966) is available in 17 reels.

Union lists of Chinese periodicals from various other countries are:

EUROPE:

P 12. *A Bibliography of Chinese Newsapapers and Periodicals*

in European Libraries. Cambridge, Eng.: Cambridge University Press, 1975.
A unique comprehensive listing of 1,025 periodicals. Note also listing of similar bibliographies in other countries on p. 7.

AUSTRALIA:

P 13. *Chinese Periodicals in the Libraries of the Australian National University, the University of Sydney and the University of Melbourne*. Canberra: Library of the Australian National University, 1973.

FRANCE:

P 14. *Périodiques en langue chinoise de la Bibliothèque Nationale*. Marie-Rose Séguy. Paris: Universite Paris-VII, 1972.

HONGKONG:

P 15. *An Annotated Guide to Current Chinese Periodicals in Hongkong*. Paul P. W. Cheng 鄭保羅. San Francisco: Chinese Materials and Research Aids Service Center, 1973.

GREAT BRITAIN:

P 16. *Chinese Periodicals in British Libraries*. Trustees of the British Museum. London, 1965, 1969, 1972.

JAPAN:

P 17. *Wa-zasshi mokuroku ko* 和雜誌目錄稿. Kokuritsu Kokkai Toshokan. Tokyo: National Diet Library, 1969.

TAIWAN:

P 18. *A Union List of Chinese Periodicals in Universities and Colleges in Taiwan*. William C. Ju 諸家駿. San Francisco: Chinese Materials Center, 1975.
Reviewed by Ernst Wolff in *Journal of Library and Information Science* 3.1:131-3 (April 1977).

NEWSPAPERS AND PERIODICALS OF HONGKONG, TAIWAN, AND MAINLAND CHINA

HONGKONG:

The main English-language newspapers in Hongkong are the *South China Morning Post* and the *Hongkong Standard*. The main Chinese newspaper is the *Hsing-tao jih-pao* 星島日報. There are innumerable periodicals of which the *Ming-pao yüeh-k'an* 明報月刊 at present enjoys greatest popularity. The main English-language periodical is the *Far Eastern Economic Review* for information on East and Southeast Asia and the *China News Analysis* for information on the mainland. Of interest, too, are the translation and monitoring services of the U.S. Consulate General: see Berton and Wu Guide [C 6], chapter X, and Andrew Nathan's *Modern China* [C 7], pp. 38-40.

TAIWAN:

The main newspapers are the *Chung-yang jih-pao* 中央日報 and the *Lien-ho pao* 聯合報. The main periodical of scholarly interest (history) is the *Tung-fang tsa-chih* 東方雜誌.

Additional references to consult:

P 19. *An Annotated Guide to Taiwan Periodical Literature*. Robert L. Irick. Taipei: Chinese Materials and Research Aids Service Center, 1972.

P 20. *Chung-hua min-kuo ch'i k'an lun wen so yin* 中華民國期刊論文索引. Taipei: National Central Library, 1970-

See also Teng and Biggerstaff, pp. 72-82.

PEOPLE'S REPUBLIC OF CHINA:

The two main newspapers are the *Jen-min jih-pao* 人民日報, the government organ, and the *Kuang-ming jih-pao* 光明日報. The latter is said to cater more to educational and intellectual circles and to report on news concerning primarily science and education, according to its editorial of 1 May 1978. There are indexes to both, see:

P 21. *Research Materials on 20th Century China; an Annotated List of CCRM Publications*. P. K. Yu 余秉權 comp., in collaboration with Ingeborg Knezevich, James Cheng, and Ping-fen Chi. Washington, D.C.: Center for Chinese Research Materials, Assoc. of Research Libraries, 1975.
In particular pp. 55-6.

The main periodical is the *Hung-ch'i* 紅旗, the political and ideological mouthpiece of the CCP. Translations of newspaper and periodical articles appear in the following publications:

P 22. *China News Analysis,* Hongkong. 25 August 1953- weekly.

P 23. Translation and Information series of the U.S. Consulate General, Hongkong. See Nathan [C 7], pp. 38-9.

P 24. Translation series of the U.S. Joint Publications Research Service (JPRS). Washington, D.C. March 1957-
Now indexed in *Transdex* by CCM Information Corpoation, New York, 1971-. For earlier indexes, see Berton and Wu Guide, pp. 411-2; also Nathan [C 7], pp. 39-40.

For further references to PRC publications, see:

P 25. *Die VR China, eine annotierte Zeitschriftenbibliographie 1960-1970.* Christine Herzer. Wiesbaden, Germany: Harrassowitz, 1971.
An annotated bibliography of mainland periodicals. A valuable listing, useful for non-German readers as well. Some limitations are discussed in the review by H. Walravens in *Asiatische Studien* 28.2:150-4 (1974).

The three most important English-language periodicals from Peking are:

P 26. *China Reconstructs*. Peking: China Welfare Institute, 1952- monthly.

P 27. *Beijing Review* (formerly "Peking Review"). Peking: Pei-ching chou-pao-she, 1958- monthly.

P 28. *Chinese Literature*. Peking: Foreign Languages Press, 1951- monthly.

For scientific periodicals in particular, see:

P 29. *Directory of Selected Scientific Institutions in Mainland China*. Surveys and Research Corporation, Washington, D.C., comp. Stanford, Calif.: Hoover Institution Press, 1970.

P 30. *International Union List of Communist Chinese Serials, Scientific, Technical and Medical*. Bernadette P. N. Shih and Richard L. Snyder. Cambridge, Mass.: M. I. T. Press, 1963.

For further references see also:

Berton and Wu Guide, chapter XVII, section C.
Teng and Biggerstaff, pp. 72-82.

Q. Yearbooks

Yearbooks on China were first published by Westerners to provide background data on the political and economic conditions of the country, mainly for the benefit of the trading community in the pre-World War II treaty ports. For example, see:

Q 1. *China Year Book.* H. G. W. Woodhead, ed. Shanghai: North China Daily News, 1912-1939.
Published annually with few interruptions. It has excellent editorial collaboration including Owen Lattimore on the border regions, E. Kann on currency and banking, J. C. Ferguson on art.

In the thirties the Chinese started the publication of yearbooks. Examples:

Q 2. *Shen-pao nien-chien* 申報年鑑. Shanghai: Shen-pao, 1933-1936 and 1944.
The last issue is particularly interesting for its information on wartime Shanghai.

Q 3. *Chinese Year Book* 中國年鑑. Shanghai: Commercial Press. 1935/36 to 1944/45 (7 vols.).
"Prepared from official sources by the Council of International Affairs, Nanking."

On more recent developments read Berton and Wu Guide [C 6], chapter IV, pp. 106-28, and Andrew Nathan [C 7], pp. 50-54. Also note:

Q 4. *Chung-hua min-kuo nien-chien* 中華民國年鑑. Published annually by the China Publishing Co., Taipei, under government auspices since 1951, with Chinese and English editions.

Yearbooks for the People's Republic started with:

Q 5. *Chung-hua jen-min kung-ho-kuo jen-min shou-ts'e* 中華人民共和國人民手冊. Yang-ch'in 羊秦. Canton: Pai-yün, 1949.
Reprinted by the Center for Chinese Research Materials, Washington, D.C., 1970.

Q 6. *Jen-min nien-chien* 人民年鑑. Hongkong: Ta-kung-pao, 1950.

The Peking government then for a time published:

Q 7. *Jen-min shou-ts'e* 人民手冊. Tientsin: Ta-kung-pao, 1951-

But the publication ceased in 1965, about which time Taiwan intelligence sources started to publish:

Q 8. *Chung-kung nien-pao* 中共年報 (formerly *Fei-ch'ing nien-pao* 匪情年報). Taipei: Institute for the Study of Chinese Communist Problems. Annual since 1967.

Particular aspects and branches of government can be researched in the many individual annual reports and yearbooks of government ministries and departments, such as, e.g., *Chiao-yü nien-chien* 教育年鑑, *Shang-hai-shih nien-chien* 上海市年鑑, etc. For a listing of such see Teng and Biggerstaff, chapter VII, "Yearbooks," on pp. 204-13, and also:

Q 9. *Chung-fa ta-hsüeh yüeh-k'an* 中法大學月刊. 9.4:95-111 (1936).

Several of these have been reprinted by the Center for Chinese Research Materials, Washington, D.C.; see newsletters no. 23 (May 1977), pp. 14-28, and no. 24 (October 1977), pp. 17-35.

R. Travel Guides

With the "opening-up" of mainland China to travellers from Western countries, a listing of a few travel guides that have been published over the past few years may not be amiss:

R 1. *China* (Nagel's Encyclopedia-Guide). Nagel Publishers, English version by Anne L. Destenay. Geneva, 1973.
A travel guide on the pattern of the old Baedeker guides, with excellent background information and useful maps.

R 2. *Travel Guide of the People's Republic of China.* Ruth Lor Malloy. New York: Morrow, 1975.
Entertaining. Travel hints with some background material. Bibliography on pp. 174-80 for more detailed reading on the PRC.

R 3. *Tourist Guide to China.* China International Travel Service and Foreign Languages Press. Peking, 1974.
Mostly illustrations with little useful text.

R 4. *Fedor's People's Republic of China.* New York: David McKay, 1979.

There is also a guide for Taiwan:

R 5. *Guide to Taipei and All Taiwan.* Joseph J. Nerbonne. Taipei, 4th ed. 1974-1976.
"What to see, where to shop, where to eat," etc.

Appendix

HARVARD-YENCHING INSTITUTE SINOLOGICAL INDEX SERIES

1. 說苑引得 Index to Shou Yuan.
2. 白虎通引得 Index to Po Hu Tung.
3. 考古質疑引得 Index to K'ao Ku Chih Yi.
4. 歷代同姓名錄引得 Index to Li Tai T'ung Hsing Ming Lu
5. 崔東壁遺書引得 Index to Ts'ui Tung-pi Yi Shu.
6. 儀禮引得附鄭注及賈疏引書引得 Index to Yi Li and to the Titles Quoted in the Commentaries.
7. 四庫全書總目及未收書目引得 Index to Ssu K'u Ch'üan Shu Tsung Mu and Wei Shou Shu Mu. 2 Vols.
8. 全上古三代秦漢三國六朝文作者引得 Index to the Authors in Ch'üan Shang Ku San Tai Ch'in Han San Ku Liu Ch'ao Wen.
9. 三十三種清代傳記綜合引得 Index to Thirty-Three Collections of Ch'ing Dynasty Biographies.
10. 藝文志二十種綜合引得 Combined Indices to Twenty Historical Bibliographies. 4 Vols.
11. 佛藏子目引得 Combined Indices to the Authors and Titles

of Books and Chapters in Four Collections of Buddhistic Literature. 3 Vols.

12. 世說新語引得 附劉注引書引得 Index to Shih Shou Hsin Yü and to the Titles Quoted in the Commentary.
13. 容齋隨筆五集綜合引得 Combined Indices to the Five Collections of Miscellaneous Notes of Hung Mai.
14. 蘇氏演義引得 侯毅編 Index to Su Shih Yen Yi.
15. 太平廣記編目及引書引得 Index to T'ai P'ing Kuang Chi.
16. 新唐書宰相世系表引得 Index to the Genealogical Tables of the Families of Chief Ministers.
17. 水經注引得 Index to the Water Classic and Commentary. 2 Vols.
18. 唐詩紀事著者引得 Index to the Authors in T'ang Shih Chi Shih.
19. 宋詩記事著者引得 Index to the Authors in Sung Shih Chi Shih.
20. 元詩記事著者引得 Index to the Authors in Yuan Shih Chi Shih.
21. 清代書畫家字號引得 Index to the Fancy Names of the Calligraphers and Painters of the Ch'ing Dynasty.
22. 刊誤引得 Index to the Rectification of Errors of Li Fou.
23. 太平御覽引得 Index to T'ai P'ing Yü Lan.
24. 八十九種明代傳記綜合引得 Combined Indices to Eighty Nine Collections of Ming Dynasty Biographies. 3 Vols.
25. 道藏子目引得 Combined Indices to the Authors and Titles of Books in Two Collections of Taoist Literature.
26. 文選注引書引得 Index to the Titles Quoted in the Commentary on Wen Hsüan.
27. 禮記引得 Index to Li Chi.
28. 藏書紀事詩引得 An Index to the Poetical History of Book Collecting.
29. 春秋經傳注疏引書引得 Combined Indices to the Titles Quoted in the Commentaries on Ch'un-ch'iu, Kung-yang, Ku-liang and Tso-chuan.
30. 禮記注疏引書引得 Index to the Titles Quoted in the Commentaries on Li Chi.

31. 毛詩注疏引書引得 Index to the Titles Quoted in the Commentaries on Shih Ching.
32. 食貨志十五種綜合引得 Combined Indices to the Economic Sections of Fifteen Standard Histories.
33. 三國志及裴注綜合引得 Combined Indices to San Kuo Chih and Notes of P'ei Sung-chih.
34. 四十七種宋代傳記綜合引得 Combined Indices to Forty-Seven Collections of Sung Dynasty Biographies.
35. 遼金元傳記三十種綜合引得 Combined Indices to Thirty Collections of Liao, Chin and Yüan Biographies.
36. 漢書及補注綜合引得 Combined Indices to Han Shu and the Notes of Yen Shih-ku and Wang Hsien-ch'ien.
37. 周禮引得 附注疏引書引得 Index to Chou Li and to the Titles Quoted in the Commentaries.
38. 爾雅注疏引書引得 Index to the Titles Quoted in the Commentaries on Erh Ya.
39. 全漢三國晉南北朝詩作者引得 Index to the Authors in Ch'üan Han San Kuo Chin Nan Pei Ch'ao Shih.
40. 史記及注釋綜合引得 Combined Indices to Shih Chi and the Notes of P'ei Yin.
41. 後漢書及注釋綜合引得 Combined Indices to Hou Hanshu and the Notes of Liu Chao and Li Hsien.

HARVARD-YENCHING INSTITUTE SINOLOGICAL INDEX SERIES, SUPPLEMENTS

1. 讀史年表附引得 Chinese Chronological Charts With Index.
2. 諸史然疑校訂附引得 Chu-shih Jan Yi re-edited and indexed.
3. 明代勅選書考附引得 Ming Tai Ch'ih Chuan Shu K'ao.
4. 引得說 On Indexing.
5. 勺園圖錄考 The Mi Garden.

6. 日本期刊三十八種中東方學論文篇目附引得 A Bibliography of Orientological Contributions in Thirty-Eight Japanese Periodicals with Indices.
7. 封氏開見記校證附引得 Miscellaneous Notes of Feng Yen. 2 Vols.
8. 清畫傳輯佚三種附引得 Biographies of Ch'ing Dynasty Painters in Three Collections.
9. 毛詩引得(附標校經文) A Concordance to Shih Ching.
10. 周易引得(附標校經文) A Concordance to Yi Ching.
11. 春秋經傳引得(附標校經傳全文) Combined Concordances to Ch'un-Ch'iu Kung-yang, Ku-liang and Tso-chuan. 4 Vols.
12. 琬琰集删存附引得 Yuan Yen Chi Abridged. 3 Vols.
13. 一百七十五種日本期刊中東方學論文篇目附引得 A Bibliography of Orientological Contributions in One Hundred and Seventy-five Japanese Periodicals with Indices.
14. 杜詩引得 A Concordance to the Poems of Tu Fu. 3 Vols.
15. 六藝之一錄目錄附引得 A Table of Contents of Liu Yi Chih Yi Lu with Index.
16. 論語引得(附標校經文) A Concordance to the Analects of Confucius.
17. 孟子引得(附標校經文) A Concordance to Meng Tzu.
18. 爾雅引得(附標校經文) Index to Erh Ya.
19. 增校清朝進士題名碑錄附引得 Chin Shih T'i Ming Pei Lu of Ch'ing Dynasty.
20. 莊子引得 A Concordance to Chuang Tzu.
21. 墨子引得 A Concordance to Mo Tzu.
22. 荀子引得 A Concordance to Hsun Tzu.
23. 孝經引得 A Concordance to Hsiao Ching.

CENTRE FRANCO-CHINOIS D'ETUDES SINOLOGIQUES

1. 論衡通檢 Index du Louen Heng.
2. 呂氏春秋通檢 Index du Liu Che Tch'ouen Ts'ieou.
3. 風俗通義附通檢 Index du Fong Sou T'ong Yi avec texte critique.
4. 春秋繁露通檢 Index du Tch'ouen Ts'ieou Fan Lou.
5. 淮南子通檢 Index du Houai Nan Tseu.
6. 潛夫論通檢 Index du Ts'ien Fou Louen.
7. 新序通檢 Index du Hsin Hsiu.
8. 申鑒通檢 Index du Chen Kien.
9. 山海經通檢 Index du Chan Hai King.
10. 戰國策通檢 Index du Tchan Kouo Ts'o.
11. 大金國志通檢 Index du Ta Kin Kouo Tche.
12. 契丹國志通檢 Index du K'i-Tan Kouo Tche.
13. 輟耕錄通檢 Index du Tcho Keng Lou.
14. 方言校箋附通檢 Index du Fang Yen, avec texte critique.
15. 文心雕龍新書附通檢 Index du Wen Sin Tiao Long, avec texte critique.
16. 尙書通檢 Index du Chang Chou.

CHINESE MATERIALS AND RESEARCH AIDS SERVICE CENTER

RESEARCH AIDS SERIES

1. *A Classified Index to Articles on Fiscal Policy (1945-65)* 財政論文分類索引, compiled by Frank K. S. Yüan 袁坤祥 and Ma Ching-hsien 馬景賢 (1967), xxxvi, 303pp. ISBN 0-89644-540-2.
2. *A Classified Index to Articles on Economics (1945-65)* 經濟論文分類索引, compiled by Frank K. S. Yüan 袁坤祥

and Ma Ching-hsien 馬景賢 (1967), 2 vols., ciii, (1), 1-792pp. + iii, (1), 793-1,742pp. ISBN 0-89644-541-0.

3. *A Classified Index to Articles on Money and Banking (1945-65)* 貨幣金融論文分類索引, compiled by Farnk K. S. Yüan 袁坤祥 and Ma Ching-hsien 馬景賢 (1967), xliii, 329pp. ISBN 0-89644-542-9.
4. *A Concordance to the Poems of Li Ho (790-816)* 李賀詩引得, compiled by Robert L. Irick 艾文博 (1969), xlii, 217pp. ISBN 0-89644-543-7.
5. *A Chinese-Mongolian Dictionary* 漢蒙字典, compiled by Harnod Hakanchulu 哈勘楚論 (1969), lxxviii, 1,536pp. ISBN 0-89644-544-5.
6. *A Typeset Edition of the Diary of weng T'ung-ho with Index* 翁同龢日記排印本附索引, edited by Chao Chung-fu 趙中孚 (1970). Text in 5 vols., 5, 1-524pp. + 525-993pp. + 995-1,522pp. + 1,523-2,002pp. + 2,003-2,448pp. Vol. 6: Index (1979), (xxvii), 400p. ISBN 0-89644-545-3.
7. *Title and Author Index to* Ts'ung-shu *in Taiwan Libraries* 臺灣各圖書館現存叢書子目索引, compiled by Wang Pao-hsien 王寶先. Part I: Title Index, 2 vols. (1976), xxi, 868pp. + ii, 740pp. Part II: Author Index (1977), xii, 190pp. ISBN 0-89644-546-1.
8. *A Typeset Edition of the* Tu-li ts'un-i 讀例存疑重刊本, edited by Huang Tsing-chia 黃靜嘉 (1970), 5 vols., 1-262pp. + 4, 1-372pp. + 2, 373-699pp. + 2, 701-1,025pp. + 2, 1,026-1,357pp. ISBN 0-89644-547-X.
9. *A Concordance to the* Kuan-tzu 管子引得, compiled by Wallace Johnson 莊爲斯 (1970), lxxviii, 1,188pp. ISBN 0-89644-548-8.
10. *Index to the Ho Collection of Twenty-Eight* Shih-hua 索引本何氏歷代詩話, compiled by Helmut Martin 馬漢茂 (1973), 2 vols.: vol. 1, xviii, 533pp.; vol. 2, 1, 860pp. ISBN 0-89644-549-6.
11. *A Concordance to the* Kuo-yü 國語引得, compiled by Wolfgang Bauer 包吾剛 (1973), 2 vols.: vol. 1, xlii, 808pp.;

vol 2, iv, 486pp. ISBN 0-89644-550-X.

12. *A Concordance to the* Jen-wu Chih *with a Text* 人物志引得, compiled by Wolfgang Bauer 包吾剛 (1974), xvi, 240pp. ISBN 0-89644-551-8.
13. *A Concordance to* Han-fei Tzu 韓非子引得, compiled by Wallace Johnson 莊爲斯 (1975), xxxix, 978pp. ISBN 0-89644-552-6.
14. *A Concordance to the Poems of Wei Ying wu* 韋應物詩注引得, compiled by Thomas P. Nielsor (1976), lxxii, 220pp. ISBN 0-89644-553-4.
15. *An Index to Sung Synasty Titles Extant in* Ts'ung-shu 叢書索引宋文子目, compiled by Brian E. McKnight (1977), xii, 373pp. ISBN 0-89644-554-2.
16. *An Annotated Guide to Documents on Sino-Japanese-Korean Relations in the Late Ch'ing Dynasty* 清季中日韓關係資料卅種綜合分類目錄, compiled by Li Yü-shu 李毓澍 (1977), 2 vols., xxxii, 1-699pp. + xxxii, 701-1,169pp. ISBN 0-89644-550-0.
17. *Modern Japanese Authors in Area Studies: A Namelist,* compiled by Austin C. W. Shu (1978), xii, 151pp. ISBN 0-89644-517-8.

IN PREPARATION

"A Index to Diplomatic Documents of the Late Ch'ing Dynasty (1875-1911) 清季外交史料引得," compiled by Robert L. Irick 艾文博.

"Index to Chinese Terms in the English Translations of Henry Doré, *Researches into Chinese Superstitions*, vols. 1-10 and 13," compiled by Anne S. Goodrich.

"Chinese Names of Foreigners in China," edited by Robert L. Irick 艾文博 and Linda Marks.

"Taiwan Publications, 1964-1974: An Index by Subject, uthor, and Title to New Works and Reprints appearing in MRASC Booklists," edited by Robert L. Irick.

CHINESE MATERIALS AND RESEARCH AIDS SERVICE CENTER

BIBLIOGRAPHICAL AIDS SERIES

1. *A Checklist of Reference Works in Teng and Biggerstaff Now Available in Taiwan* (1970), 2, 33pp. Paperbound. ISBN 0-89644-199-7.
2. Lei Shu: *Old Chinese Reference Works and a Checklist of Cited Titles Available in Taiwan*, compiled by Austin C. W. Shu (1973), xvii, 37pp. Paperbound. ISBN 0-89644-527-5.
3. *A Descriptive Catalog of the Ming Editions in the Far Eastern Library of the University of Washington,* compiled by Chik-fong Lee (1975), xvii, 53pp. Paperbound. ISBN 0-89644-425-2.
4. *Chinese Folk Narratives: A Bibliographical Guide*, compiled by Nai-tung Ting and Lee-hsia Hsü Ting (1975), xiii, 68pp. Paperbound. ISBN 0-89644-434-1.

CHINESE MATERIALS CENTER

RESEARCH AIDS SERIES

1. *Research Guide to the* Chiao-hui hsin-pao ("The Church News"), *1868-1874* 教會新報目錄導要, compiled by Adrian A. Bennett (1975), xviii, 342pp. ISBN 0-89644-528-3.
2. *Research Guide to the* Wan-kuo kung-pao ("The Globe Magazine"), *1874-1883* 萬國公報目錄導要, compiled by Adrian A. Bennett (1976), xvi, 519pp. ISBN 0-89644-529-1.
3. Ku Hung-ting 古鴻廷, *The Grand Secretariat in Ch'ing China: A Chronological List* 清代大學士年表(1980), (viii), xi, 151pp. ISBN 0-89644-630-1.
4. Lee Chik-fong 李直方, *Index to Pre-T'ang Poetry: A Combined Index to* Ku shih yüan *and* Ku shih hsüan 古詩索引 (1980), (iv), xxvi, 135pp. ISBN 0-89644-631-X.

CHINESE MATERIALS CENTER

BIBLIOGRAPHIC SERIES

Robert L. Irick, General Editor

1. Wolff, Ernest, *Chinese Studies: A Bibliographic Manual* (1981), xiv, 152pp. ISBN 0-89644-627-1
3. *Books on China, 1980: A Cumulative List with Descriptions of Original and Reprinted Western-Language Titles Available from Taiwan* (1980), viii, 308pp. ISBN 0-89644-629-8

CHINESE MATERIALS CENTER

CHINA PROBLEM SERIES

Robert L. Irick, General Editor

1. Lee, Orlan, *Bureaucratic Despotism and Reactionary Revolution: The Ideological Significance of Wittfogel's Concept of Oriental Despotism* (1981), viii, 85pp. ISBN 0-89644-638-7
2. Hsü, Cho-yun, *Bibliographic Notes on the Studies of Early China* (1981), viii, 88pp. ISBN 0-89644-637-9

CHINESE MATERIALS CENTER

ASIAN LIBRARY SERIES

Robert L. Irick, General Editor

1. *Translations from Po Chü-i's Collected Works: III, Regulated and Patterned Poems of Middle Age (822-832),* translated and described by Howard S. Levy, rendered by Henry W. Wells (1976), xxxiv, 215pp. ISBN 0-89644-463-5.
2. *Translations from Po Chü-i's Collected Works: IV, The Later Years (833-846),* translated and described by Howard S. Levy, rendered by Henry W. Wells (1978), li, 711pp. ISBN 0-89644-518-6.
3. Marney, John, *A Handbook of Modern Chinese Grammar* (1977), 78pp. Paperbound. ISBN 0-89644-464-3.
4. Wells, Henry W., tr., *Diary of a Pilgrim to Ise,* attributed to Saka Jūbutsu, with illustrations by Ch'eng Hsi (1977), xii, 135pp. Paperbound. ISBN 0-89644-501-1.
5. Teng Shou-hsin, *A Basic Course in Chinese Grammar: A Graded Approach through* Conversational Chinese (1977), xii, 135pp. Paperbound. ISBN 0-89644-502-X.
6. Carrington, George Williams, *Foreigners in Formosa, 1841-1874* (1977), frontis., map, index, xiv, 308pp. ISBN 0-89644-506-2.
7. Lee, Orlan, *Legal and Moral Systems in Asian Customary Law: The Legacy of the Buddhist Social Ethic and Buddhist Law* (1978), map, index, xxiv, 456pp. ISBN 0-89644-524-0.
8. Miao, Ronald C., ed., *Chinese Poetry and Poetics, Vol. 1* (1978), xiv, 375pp. ISBN 0-89644-525-9.
9. Sailey, Jay, *The Master Who Embraces Simplicity: A Study of the Chinese Philosopher, Ko Hung, A.D. 283-343* (1978), index, xxvi, 658pp. ISBN 0-89644-522-4.
10. Pruitt, Ida, *A China Childhood* (1978), xi, 205pp. ISBN 0-89644-523-2.
11. Kracke, Edward A., Jr., *Translations of Sung Civil Service Titles, Classification Terms, and Governmental Organ Names,* rev. ed. (1978), xiii, 35pp. ISBN 0-89644-526-7.
12. Lee, Yu-hwa, *The Last Rite and Other Stories* (1979), xviii, 303pp. ISBN 0-89644-574-7.
13. Allan, Sarah and Alvin P. Cohen, *Legend, Lore, and Religion in China: Essays in Honor of Wolfram Eberhard on His Seventieth Birthday* (1979), frontis, xxiv, 269pp. ISBN 0-89644-584-4.
14. Hsieh, Shan-yüan, *The Life and Thought of Li Kou, 1009-1059* (1979), viii, 228pp. chart. ISBN 0-89644-586-0.
15. Ing, Nancy, tr. an ed. *New Voices: Stories and Poems by Young Chinese Writers,* 2nd ed. (1980), xii, 212pp. ISBN 0-89644-580-1.

IN PREPARATION

Robert L. Irick, "Ch'ing Policy Toward the Coolie Trade, 1847-1878."

Edward Gerald Martinique, "Chinese Traditional Bookbinding: A Study of its Evolution and Techniques."

Arnold J. Meagher, "Introduction of Chinese Laborers to Latin America: The 'Coolie Trade,' 1847-1874."

Ronald C. Miao, "The Life and Lyric Poetry of Wang Ts'an, 177-217."

Constance Miller, "Technical and Cultural Prerequisites for the Invention of Printing in China and the West."

Shiow-jyu Lu Shaw, "The Imperial Printing of Early Ch'ing China, 1644-1805."

Paul Vander Meer, "Farm-plot Dispersal: Lu-liao Village, Taiwan, 1967."

Sailey Min chih Yao, "The Influence of Chinese and Japanese Calligraphy on Mark Tobey (1890-1976)."

Peter Lum, "My Own Pair of Wings."

Nancy Ing, "Winter Plum: Selected Fiction from Contemporary Taiwan"

THE
STANFORD
CHINESE CONCORDANCE SERIES

David S. Nivison, Editor

Volume 1

No. 1: *A Concordance to Chu Hsi, "Ta Hsüeh Chang Chü,"* comp. P. J. Ivanhoe, prog. Margaret Waters (1979), xviii, (98)p.

No. 2: *A Concordance to Chu Hsi, "Chung Yung Chang Chü,"* comp. P. J. Ivanhoe, prog. Margaret Waters (1979), (vi), (190)p.

Volume 2

No. 3:1: *A Concordance to Wang Yang-ming, "Ch'uan Hsi Lu": Text*, comps. P. J. Ivanhoe, David S. Nivison, Peter K. Meic, prog. Margaret Waters (1979), xxvi, (428)p.

Volume 3

No. 3:2: *A Concordance to Wang Yang-ming, "Ch'uan Hsi Lu": Concordance*, comps. P. J. Ivanhoe, David S. Nivison, Peter K. Meic, prog. Margaret Waters (1979), xxvi, (510)p.

No. 4. *A Concordance to Wang Yang-ming, "Ta Hsüeh Wen,"* comp. P. J. Ivanhoe, prog. Margaret Waters (1979), (iv), (42)p.

Volume 4

No. 5: *A Concordance to Tai Chen, "Yüan Shan,"* comp. P. J. Ivanhoe, prog. Margaret Waters (1979), xxviii, (152)p.

No. 6. *A Concordance to Tai Chen, "Meng Tzu Tzu I Shu Cheng,"* comps. P. J. Ivanhoe, David S. Nivison, prog. Margaret Waters (1979), (vi), (496)p.

CHINESE MATERIALS CENTER

RESEARCH AIDS SERIES

Robert L. Irick, General Editor

1. *Research Guide to the* Chiao-hui hsin-pao ("The Church News"), *1868-1874* 教會新報目錄導要, compiled by Adrian A. Bennett (1975), xviii, 342pp. ISBN 0-89644-528-3.
2. *Research Guide to the* Wan-kuo kung-pao ("The Globe Magazine"), *1874-1883* 萬國公報目錄導要, compiled by Adrian A. Bennett (1976), xvi, 519pp. ISBN 0-89644-529-1.
3. Ku Hung-ting 古鴻廷, *The Grand Secretariat in Ch'ing China: A Chronological List* 清代大學士年表 (1980), (viii), vi, 151pp. ISBN 0-89644-630-1.
4. Lee Chik-fong 李直方, *Index to Pre-T'ang Poetry: A Combined Index to* Ku shih yüan *and* Ku shih hsüan 古詩索引 (1980), (iv), xxvi, 135pp. ISBN 0-89644-631-X.

CHINESE MATERIALS CENTER

REPRINT SERIES

1. Lewis, Ida Belle, *The Education of Girls in China* (San Francisco: CMC, 1974; Repr. of New York: Teachers College, Columbia University, 1919), (xii), 92pp., 1 folding map.
2. Beal, Samuel, intro. and tr., *The Life of Hiuen-Tsiang by the Shaman Hwui Li* (San Francisco: CMC, 1974; Repr. of London: Kegan, Paul, Trench, Trübner & Co., 1911), (ii), xlviii, 218pp.
3. Giles, Herbert A., tr., *Strange Stories from a Chinese Studio* (San Francisco: CMC, 1974; Repr. of London: T. Werner Laurie, 1916), (ii), xxiv, 488pp.
4. Morse, H.B., *In the Days of the Taipings* (San Francisco: CMC, 1974; Repr. of Salem: The Essex Institute, 1927), frontis., (iv), xiv, 434pp.
5. Howard, Harvey J., *Ten Weeks with Chinese Bandits* (San Francisco: CMC, 1974; Repr. of New York: Dodd, Mead and Company, 1927), frontis., (ii), xxxiv, 399pp., 1 folding map.
6. Hall, W.H. & W.D. Bernard, *The* Nemesis *in China* (San Francisco: CMC, 1974; Repr. of London: Henry Colburn, 1847), (iv), xvi, 272pp.
7. Thomson, John, *Through China with a Camera* (San Francisco: CMC, 1974; Repr. of Westminister: A. Constable & Co., 1898), (ii), xiv, 284pp.
8. Duyvendak, J.J.L., tr. and ed., *The Book of Lord Shang* (San Francisco: CMC, 1974; Repr. of London: Arthur Probstain, 1928), (ii), xvi, 346pp.
9. Kerr, John Glasgow, *A Guide to the City and Suburbs of Canton* (San Francisco: CMC, 1974; Repr. of Hong Kong: Kelly and Walsh, 1918), viii, 103pp. 1 folding map.
10. Grey, John Henry, *Walks in the City of Canton* (San Francisco: CMC, 1974; Repr. of Hong Kong: De Souza & Co., 1875), (vi), vi, 695, lxipp.
11. des Rotours, Robert, *Traité des fonctionnaires et Traité de l'Armeé* (San Francisco: CMC, 1974; Repr. of 2nd ed.—revised and corrected [Leiden: E.J. Brill, 1948]), cxx, 499 + (iv), 594 (ii)pp., 9 folding maps, 1 folding chart, 2 v.
12. Burns, Islay, *Memoir of the Reverend William C. Burns, M. A., Missionary to China from the English Presbyterian Church* (San Francisco: CMC, 1975; Repr. of New York: Robert Carter and Brothers, 1870), (viii), viii, 595pp.
13. *Report of the Advisory Committee Together with Other Documents Respecting the Chinese Indemnity* (San Francisco: CMC, 1975; Repr. of London: Her Majesty's Stationery Office, 1926), (ii), 197pp.
14. *Report of the Commission of Extraterritoriality in China* (San Francisco: CMC, 1975; Repr. of London: His Majesty's Stationery Office, 1926), (ii), 130pp.
15. Beale, Louis & G. Clinton, *Trade and Economic Conditions in China, 1931-1933, Together with an Annex on Trading Conditions in Manchuria* (San Francisco: CMC, 1975; Repr. of London: His Majesty's Stationery Office, 1933), (ii), 174pp., 1 folding map.

16. *Report on the Trade of Central and Southern China* (San Francisco: CMC, 1975; Repr. of London: His Majesty's Stationery Office, 1898), (ii), 99pp.
17. *Papers Relating to the Riot in Canton in July 1846 and to the Proceedings Against Mr. Compton, a British Subject, for His Participation in That Riot* (San Francisco: CMC, 1975; Repr. of London: T.R. Harrison, 1847), (ii), vi, 130pp.
18. *Correspondence Respecting Insults in China* (San Francisco: CMC, 1975; Repr. of London: Harrison and Sons, 1857), (ii), viii, 228pp.
19. *Correspondence Respecting Anti-foreign Riots in China, 1891-1892* (San Francisco: CMC, 1975; Repr. of London: Her Majesty's Stationery Office, 1891), (iv), 176pp.
20. *Correspondence Respecting the Attack on British Protestant Missionaries at Yang-chow-foo, August 1868* (San Francisco: CMC, 1975; Repr. of London: Harrison and Sons, 1869), (ii), iv, 78, (4) 18pp.
21. *Correspondence Respecting the Attack on the Indian Expedition to Western China, and the Murder of Mr. Margary* (San Francisco: CMC, 1975; Repr. of London: Harrison and Sons, 1876, 1877), (ii), iv, 148pp.
22. *Papers Relating to the Rebellion in China and Trade in the Yang-tze-kiang River* (San Francisco: CMC, 1975; Repr. of London: Harrison and Sons, 1862), (ii), iv, 158pp. 1 folding map.
23. *Further Papers Relating to the Rebellion in China* (San Francisco: CMC, 1975; Repr. of London: Harrison and Sons, 1863), (iv), 196pp.
24. Hamberg, Theodore, *The Visions of Hung-siu-tshuen and Origin of the Kwang-si Insurrection* (San Francisco: CMC, 1975; Repr. of Hong Kong: China Mail Office, 1854), (iv), vi, 63, (i), xiipp.
25. *Foreign Relations of the United States, 1901: Affairs in China. Report of William W. Rockhill, Late Commissioner to China, with Accompanying Documents* (San Francisco: CMC, 1975; Repr. of China reprint edition, 1941), (ii), 391pp.
26. *Correspondence Respecting the Revision of the Treaty of Tien-tsin* (San Francisco: CMC, 1975; Repr. of London: Harrison and Sons, 1871), (ii), viii, 467pp.
27. Allman, Norwood F., *Handbook on the Protection of Trade-marks, Patents, Copyrights, and Trade-names in China* (San Francisco: CMC, 1975; Repr. of Shanghai: Kelly & Walsh, 1924), (vi), iv, 207, 5pp.
28. Hsia, Ching-lin, *Studies in Chinese Diplomatic History* (San Francisco: CMC, 1975; Repr. of Shanghai: Commercial Press, 1925), (ii) xii, 266, 4pp.
29. Song Ong Siang, *One Hundred Years' History of the Chinese in Singapore; Being a Chronological Record of the Contribution by the Chinese Community to the Development, Progress and Prosperity of Singapore; of Events and Incidents Concerning the Whole or Sections of That Community and of the Lives, Pursuits and Public Service of Individual Members Thereof from the Foundation of Singapore on 6th February 1919* (San Francisco: CMC, 1975; Repr. of London: John Murray, 1923), (iv), xxii, 602pp.
30. Sargent, A.J., *Anglo-Chinese Commerce and Diplomacy (Mainly in the Nineteenth Century)* (San Francisco: CMC, 1975; Repr. of Oxford: Clar-

endon Press, 1907), frontis., xii, 332pp.
31. Rasmussen, O.D., *What's Right with China: An Answer to Foreign Criticisms* (San Francisco: CMC, 1975; Repr. of Shanghai: Commercial Press, 1927), (ii) xx, 255pp.
32. Soothill, W.E., *China and the West: A Sketch of Their Intercourse* (San Francisco: CMC, 1975; Repr. of London: Humphrey Milford, 1925), frontis., (iv), viii, 216pp.
33. Arnold, Julean, et al., *Commercial Handbook of China* (San Francisco: CMC, 1975; Repr. of US Dept. of Commerce, Bureau of Foreign and Domestic Commerce, Miscellaneous Series No. 84 [Washington: Government Printing Office, 1919]), frontis., (ii), 630pp., 2 folding maps. + frontis., (ii) 470pp. 2v.
34. *Correspondence Respecting the Disturbances in China,* China No. 1, and *Further Correspondence Respecting the Disturbances in China,* China Nos. 5 & 6 (San Francisco: CMC, 1975; Repr. of London: His Majesty's Stationery Office, 1901), (ii), xxiv, 200 + (ii), xvi, 162 + xiv, 175pp. For the first volume of documents on this subject, see no. 90.
35. *Correspondence Relative to the Earl of Elgin's Special Missions to China and Japan, 1857-1859* (San Francisco: CMC, 1975; Repr. of London: Harrison and Sons, 1859), (ii), xii, 488pp.
36. Legge, James, tr., *A Record of Buddhistic Kingdoms: Being an Account by the Chinese Monk Fâ-Hien of His Travels in India and Ceylon (A.D. 399-414) in Search of the Buddhist Books of Discipline* (San Francisco: CMC, 1975; Repr. of Oxford: Clarendon Press, 1886), (iv), vx, (i), 123, (45)pp., 1 folding map.
37. Tucci, G., *On Some Aspects of the Doctrines of Maitreya [Nātha] and Asaṅga (Being a Course of Five Lectures Delivered at the University of Calcutta)* (San Francisco: CMC, 1975; Repr. of Calcutta: Univ. of Calcutta, 1930), (viii), 82, 2pp.
38. Watters, Thomas, *On Yuan Chwang's Travels in India, 629-645 A.D.* (San Francisco: CMC, 1975; Repr. of London: Royal Asiatic Society, 1904), (ii), xvi, 401 + vi, 357pp., 2 folding maps. 2v.
39. Nanjio, Bunyiu, *A Catalogue of the Chinese Buddhist Tripitaka: the Sacred Canon of the Buddhists in China and Japan* (San Francisco: CMC, 1975; Repr. of Oxford: Clarendon Press, 1893), xxxvi, 480 columns.
40. Beal, Samuel, Si-yu-ki: *Buddhist Records of the Western World; Translated from the Chinese of Hiuen Tsiang (A.D. 629)* (San Francisco: CMC, 1976; Repr. of London: Kegan Paul, Trench, Trübner & Co., n.d.), (ii), cxii, 242 + viii, 369pp. 2v. in 1.
41. Rockhill, W. Woodville, tr., *The Life of the Buddha and the Early History of His Order; Derived from Tibetan Works in the* Bkah-Hgyur *and* Bstan-Hgyur; *Followed by Notices on the Early History of Tibet and Khoten* (San Francisco: CMC, 1976; Repr. of London: Kegan Paul, Trench, Trübner & Co., Introduction dated June 1884), xii, 273pp.
42. Edkins, Joseph, *Chinese Buddhism: A Volume of Sketches, Historical, Descriptive, and Critical* (San Francisco: CMC, 1976; Repr. of Trübner's

Oriental Series, 2nd rev. ed. [London: Kegan Paul, Trench, Trübner, & Co., 1893]), (ii), xxxiv, 453pp.

43. Grousset, Réné, *In the Footsteps of the Buddha*, tr. from the French by Mariette Leon (San Francisco: CMC, 1976; Repr. of London: George Routledge & Sons, 1932), (ii), xii, 352pp., 2 folding maps.

44. Mateer, A.H., *Siege Days: Personal Experiences of American Women and Children During the Peking Siege* (San Francisco: CMC, 1976; Repr. of New York: Fleming H. Revell Co., 1903), (ii), 411pp.

45. Eitel, Ernest J., *Hand-book of Chinese Buddhism; Being a Sanskrit-Chinese Dictionary with Vocabularies of Buddhist Terms in Pali, Singhalese, Siamese, Burmese, Tibetan, Mongolian and Japanese* (San Francisco: CMC, 1976; Repr. of 2nd rev. and enl. ed. [Tokyo: Sanshusha, 1904]), (x), 324pp.

46. Suzuki, Teitaro, *Acvaghosha's Discourse on the Awakening of Faith in the Mathâyâna* 大乘起信論 (San Francisco: CMC, 1976; Repr. of Chicago: Open Court Publishing Co., 1900), (ii), xviii, 160pp.

47. Taam, Cheuk-Woon 譚卓垣, *The Development of Chinese Libraries under the Ch'ing Dynasty, 1644-1911* 清代圖書館發展史 (San Francisco: CMC, 1977; Repr. of Shanghai, 1935), ix, 107pp.

48. Johnston, Reginald Fleming, *Buddhist China* (San Francisco: CMC, 1976; Repr. of London: John Murray, 1913), (vi), xviii, 403pp.

49. des Rotours, Robert, *Le Traité des Examens, Traduit de la Nouvelle Histoire des T'ang (Chap. XLIV, XLV)* (San Francisco: CMC, 1976; Repr. of 2nd ed.—revised and corrected [Paris: Librairie Ernest Leroux, 1932]), (ii), xii, 417pp.

50. Tucci, Giuseppe, *Pre-Dinnāga Buddhist Texts on Logic from Chinese Sources* (San Francisco: CMC, 1976; Repr. of Gaekwad's Oriental Series No. XLIX [Baroda: Oriental Institute, 1929]), (viii), xxx, 338pp.

51. Tucci, Giuseppe, *The Nyāyamukha of Dignāga, the Oldest Buddhist Text on Logic, After Chinese and Tibetan Materials* (San Francisco: CMC, 1976; Repr. of Heidelberg: O. Harrassowitz, 1930), (vi), 72pp.

52. Rosenberg, Otto, *Die Probleme der Buddhistischen Philosophie*, tr. by E. Rosenberg (San Francisco: CMC, 1976; Repr. of Heidelberg: O. Harrassowitz, 1924), (ii), xvi, 287pp.

53. Kitayama, Junyu, *Metaphysik des Buddhismus, Versuch Einer Philosophischen Interpretation der Lehre Vasubandhus und Seiner Schule* (San Francisco: CMC, 1976; Repr. of Stuttgart, Berlin: Verlag Von W. Kohlhammer, 1934), (ii), xvi, 268pp.

54. Waldschmidt, Ernst, *Gandhara Kutscha Turfan, Eine Einführung in die Frühmittelalterliche Kunst Zentralasiens* (San Francisco: CMC, 1976; Repr. of Leipzig: Klinkhardt & Biermann, 1925), (ii), 116pp., 66 pages of photos.

55. Sōgen, Yamakami, *Systems of Buddhistic Thought* (San Francisco: CMC, 1976; Repr. of Calcutta: University of Calcutta, 1912), (ii), xx, 316, xxxvipp.

56. von Zach, E., tr., *Yang Hsiung's* Fa-yen *(Worte Strenger Ermahnung) ein Philosophischer Traktat aus dem Beginn der Christlichen Zeitrechnung*

(San Francisco: CMC, 1976; Repr. of Sinologische Beiträge IV [Batavia: Drukkerij Lux, 1939]), (viii), 74pp.

57. Pfister, Louis, *Notices Biographiques et Bibliographiques sur les Jesuites de l'Ancienne Mission de Chine, 1552-1773* (San Francisco: CMC, 1976; Repr. of Variétés Sinologiques Nos. 59 & 60 [Shanghai: Imprimerie de la Mission Catholique, 1932, 1934]), (vi), xxvi, 561, 6 + (vi), x, 547, 38pp. 2v. in 1.

58. Beal, Samuel, tr., *Texts from the Buddhist Canon, Commonly Known as Dhammapada, with Accompanying Narratives* (San Francisco: CMC, 1977; Repr. of Boston: Houghton, Osgood & Co., 1878), (iv), viii, 176pp.

59. Nyanatiloka, *Buddhist Dictionary: Manual of Buddhist Terms and Doctrines* (San Francisco: CMC, 1977; Repr. of Island Hermitage Publication No. 1 [Colombo: Frewin & Co., 1950]), (vi), vi, 190pp., 1 folding diagram.

60. McGovern, William Montgomery, *A Manual of Buddhist Philosophy, Vol. I Cosmology* (San Francisco: CMC, 1977; Repr. of London: Kegan Paul, Trench, Trübner & Co., New York: E.P. Dutton & Co., 1923), (x), 205pp.

61. Soothill, W.E. *The Lotus of the Wonderful Law or the Lotus Gospel: Saddharma Pundarika Sūtra, Miao-fa Lien Hua Ching* (San Francisco: CMC, 1977; Repr. of Oxford: Clarendon Press: 1930), frontis., (ii), xii, 275pp.

62. Herrmann, Albert, *Die Alten Seidenstraſsen Zwischen China und Syrien: Beiträge zur Alten Geographie Asiens, I. Abteilung, Einleitung, die Chinesischen Quellen, Zentralasien nach Ssĕ-ma Ts'ien und den Annalen der Han-Dynastie* (San Francisco: CMC, 1977; Repr. of Berlin: Weidmannsche Buchhandlung: 1910), (ii), viii, 130pp., 1 folding map.

63. Wilson, Andrew, *The "Ever-Victorious Army": A History of the Chinese Campaign under Lt.-Col. G. G. Gordon, C. B. R. E., and of the Suppression of the Tai-Ping Rebellion.* A Reprint Edition with Marginal Notes by Capt. John Holland (San Francisco: CMC, 1977; Repr. of Edinburgh & London: William Blackwood and Sons: 1868), (vi), xxxii, 396 + 397-410pp., 1 folding map.

64. Ui, H., *The Vaiśesika Philosophy According to the Daśapadārtha-Sāstra: Chinese Text, with Introduction, Translation, and Notes,* ed. by F. W. Thomas (San Francisco: CMC, 1977; Repr. of Oriental Translation Fund, New Series Vol. xxiv [London: Royal Asiatic Society: 1917]), (iv), xii, 265pp.

65. Waddell, L. Austine, *The Buddhism of Tibet or Lamaism, with Its Mystic Cults, Symbolism and Mythology, and in Its Relation to Indian Buddhism* (San Francisco: CMC, 1977; Repr. of London: W.H. Allen & Co., 1895), frontis., (ii), xx, 598pp.

66. Medhurst, W.H., *The Foreigner in Far Cathay* (San Francisco: CMC, 1977; Repr. of London: Edward Stanford, 1872), (xii), 192pp., 1 map.

67. Dennys, N.B., ed., *The Treaty Ports of China and Japan: A Complete Guide to the Open Ports of Those Countries, Together with Peking, Yedo, Hongkong, and Macao, Forming a Guide Books & Vade Mecum for Travellers, Merchants, and Residents in General* (San Francisco: CMC, 1977; Repr. of London: Trübner and Co., 1867), (iv), viii, (2), 668pp., xl, 26

appendixes, 24 folding maps, 4 maps, 1 diagram.

68. Der Ling, Princess, *Two Years in the Forbidden City* (San Francisco: CMC, 1977; Repr. of New York: Moffat, Yard & Co., 1912), frontis., (ii), ix, (5) 383pp., 17 pl.

69. Broomhall, Marshall, *The Bible in China* (San Francisco: CMC, 1977; Repr. of London: The Religious Tract Society, 1934), (vi), xvi, 190, (2)pp.

70. Bryson, Mary F., *John Kenneth Mackenzie, Medical Missionary to China* (San Francisco: CMC, 1977; Repr. of London: Hodder & Stoughton, 1891), frontis., (iv), xv, (1), 404pp.

71. Stauffer, Milton T., *The Christian Occupation of China: A General Survey of the Numerical Strength and Geographical Distributon[sic] of the Christian Forces in China, Made by the Special Committee on Survey and Occupation, China Continuation Committee, 1918-1921* (San Francisco: CMC, 1979; Repr. of Shanghai: China Continuation Committee, 1922), (vi), 14, 469, cxiipp.

72. MacGillivray, D., *A Century of Protestant Missions in China (1807-1907), Being the Centenary Conference Historical Volume* (San Francisco: CMC, 1979; Repr. of Shanghai: American Presbyterian Mission Press, 1907), (iv), viii, 678, xl, 52pp., 1 map.

73. *Musings of a Chinese Mystic: Selections from the Philosophy of Chuang Tzu,* with an Introduction by Lionel Giles (San Francisco: CMC, 1977; Repr. of the Wisdom of the East Series [London: John Murray, n.d.]), (ii), 112pp.

74. Mullie, Jos., *The Structural Principles of the Chinese Language, An Introduction to the Spoken Language (Northern Pekingese Dialect),* tr. by A. Omer Versichel (San Francisco: CMC, 1977; Repr. of Peiping: the Bureau of Engraving & Printing, 1932), (viii), xxxiv, 566, (2)pp., 1 chart. + (viii), 691, (2) pp. 2v.

75. Guinness, M. Geraldine, *The Story of the China Inland Mission* (San Francisco: CMC, 1977; Repr. of London: Morgan & Scott, 1897, 1900), frontis., (iv), xviii, 476pp., 1 folding map. + (iv), xii, 512pp., 1 folding map. 2v.

76. Broomhall, Marshall, *The Jubilee Story of the China Inland Mission, with Portraits, Illustrations & Map* (San Francisco: CMC, 1977; Repr. of London: Morgan & Scott, 1915), frontis., (iv), xvi, 386pp., 1 folding map.

77. De Groot, J.J.M., *Les Fêtes Annuellement Célébrées à Émoui (Amoy), Étude Concernant la Religion Populaire des Chinois,* tr. by C.G. Chavannes, Annales du Musée Guimet Tome Douzième, with a new Introduction by Inez de Beauclair and Harvey Molé (San Francisco: CMC, 1977; Repr. of Paris: Ernest Leroux, Editeur, 1886), frontis., xxiv, xxvi, 400pp. + frontis., (iv), vi, 401-832pp., 24 illus. 2v.

78. Hedin, Sven, *Across the Gobi Desert,* tr. H. J. Cant (San Francisco: CMC, 1977; Repr. of New York: E. P. Dutton & Company, 1932), frontis., (iv), 402pp., 114 illus., 1 map, 2 folding maps.

79. Johnson, Samuel, *Oriental Religions and Their Relation to Universal Religion: China* (San Francisco: CMC, 1978; Repr. of Boston: James R. Osgood

& Co., 1877), (iv), xxiv, 975pp.

80. Sirr, Henry Charles, *China and the Chinese: Their Religion, Character, Customs, and Manufactures: The Evils Arising from the Opium Trade: with A Glance at Our Religious, Moral, Political, and Commercial Intercourse with the Country* (San Francisco: CMC, 1978; Repr. of London: Wm. S. Orr & Co., 1849), frontis., (iv), xvi, 448pp. + frontis., (iv), viii, 443pp. 2v.

81. *List of the Higher Metropolitan and Provincial Authorities of China, Corrected to December 31st, 1885* (San Francisco: CMC, 1978; Repr. of Peking: Pei-t'ang Press, 1886), (iv), 20pp.

82. Mayers, S.F., *List of the Higher Metropolitan and Provincial Authorities of China (with Generalogical Table of the Imperial Family), Compiled by the Chinese Secretaries, H.B.M. Legation, Peking, Corrected to June 1st, 1907* (San Francisco: CMC, 1978; Repr. of Shanghai: Kelly and Walsh, 1907), folding chart, (x), 50pp.

83. *Who's Who of American Returned Students* 遊美同學錄 (San Francisco: CMC, 1978; Repr. of Peking: Tsing Hua College, 1917), (vii), v, viii, vi, 215, iv, ivpp.

84. Mackie, J. Milton, *Life of Tai-ping-wang, Chief of the Chinese Insurrection* (San Francisco: CMC, 1978; Repr. of New York: Dix, Edwares & Co., 1857), frontis., (ii), xii, 371pp.

85. Gillis, I.V. and Yü Ping-yüeh, comp., *Supplementary Index to Giles' "Chinese Biographical Dictionary"* (San Francisco: CMC, 1978; Repr. of Peiping: 1936), (viii), 86pp.

86. Löwenthal, Rudolf, *The Religious Periodical Press in China,* with 7 maps and 16 charts (San Francisco: CMC, 1978; Repr. of Sinological Series No. 57 [Peking: The Synodal Commission in China, 1940]), (viii), vi, 294pp.

87. *Who's Who in the Far East, 1906-7 June* (San Francisco: CMC, 1979; Repr. of London: Japan Press), (viii), 352, (56)pp.

88. *Who's Who in the Far East, 1907-8 June* (San Francisco: CMC, 1979; Repr. of Hong Kong: China Mail), (xxxviii), 352, (24)pp.

89. Cordier, Henri, *L'Imprimerie Sino-Européenne en Chine, Bibliographie des Ouvrages Publiés en Chine par les Européens Au XVII*^{E} *et au XVIII*^{E} *Siècle* (San Francisco: CMC, 1979; Repr. of Paris: Imprimerie Nationale, 1901), (iv), x, 76, 32, (24)pp. 3 foldings.

90. *Correspondence Respecting the Insurrectionary Movement in China, Presented to Both Houses of Parliament by Command of Her Majesty, July 1900,* China No. 3 (San Francisco: CMC, 1979; Repr. of London: Her Majesty's Stationery Office, 1900), (iv), xvi, 115pp. For the second, third, and fourth volumes of documents on this subject, see no. 34.

CHINESE MATERIALS AND RESEARCH AIDS SERVICE CENTER

BIBLIOGRAPHICAL AIDS SERIES

Robert L. Irick, General Editor

1. *A Checklist of Reference Works in Teng and Biggerstaff Now Available in Taiwan* (1970), 2, 33pp. Paperbound. ISBN 0-89644-199-7.
2. Lei Shu: *Old Chinese Reference Works and a Checklist of Cited Titles Available in Taiwan*, compiled by Austin C. W. Shu (1973), xvii, 37pp. Paperbound. ISBN 0-89644-527-5.
3. *A Descriptive Catalog of the Ming Editions in the Far Eastern Library of the University of Washington*, compiled Chik-fong Lee (1975), xvii, 53pp. Paperbound. ISBN 0-89644-425-2.
4. *Chinese Folk Narratives: A Bibliographical Guide*, compiled by Nai-tung Ting and Lee-hsia Hsü Ting (1975), xiii, 68pp. Paperbound. ISBN 0-89644-434-1.

SERIES COMPLETED

CHINESE MATERIALS AND RESEARCH AIDS SERVICE CENTER

OCCASIONAL SERIES

Robert L. Irick, General Editor

1. *An Annotated Guide to Taiwan Periodical Literature, 1966*, edited by Robert L. Irick (1966). Out of print. (See No. 15 below.)
2. *A Ming Directory—1968*, compiled by Ronald Dimberg, Edward L. Farmer, and Robert L. Irick (1968). Out of print.
3. Wan, Grace, *A Guide to* Gwoyeu Tsyrdean (1969). Paperbound, 43pp. ISBN 0-89644-134-2.
4. *"Nothing Concealed": Essays in Honor of Liu Yü-yün*, edited by Frederick Wakeman, Jr. (1970), xv, 221pp. ISBN 0-89644-198-9.
5. Eberhard, Wolfram, *Sternkunde und Weltbild in Alten China: Gesammelte Aufsätze* (1971), 417pp. ISBN 0-89644-203-9.
6. Eberhard, Wolfram, *Moral and Social Values of the Chinese: Collected Essays* (1972), xiv, 506pp. ISBN 0-89644-356-6.
7. Chan, David B., *The Usurpation of the Prince of Yen, 1403-1424* (1976), xi, 173pp. ISBN 0-89644-457-0.
8. *An Author-Title Index to* Ch'üan Han San-kuo Chin Nan Pei-ch'ao Shih 全漢三國晉南北朝詩篇名目錄, compiled by Mei-lan Marney (1973), 160pp. ISBN 0-89644-530-5.
9. *Modern Chinese Authors: A List of Pseudonyms*, compiled by Austin C. W. Shu, 2nd revised and enlarged edition (1973). ISBN 0-89644-531-3.
10. *An Annotated Guide to Current Chinese Periodicals in Hong Kong*, compiled by Paul P. W. Cheng (1973), xii, 71pp. ISBN 0-89644-358-2.
11. Day, Clarence Burton, *Career in Cathay* (1975), 185pp. ISBN 0-89644-420-1.
12. *Vietnamese, Cambodian, and Laotian Newspapers: An International Union List*, compiled by G. Raymond Nunn and Do Van Anh (1973), xiii, 104pp. ISBN 0-89644-532-1.
13. *Burmese and Thai Newspapers: An International Union List*, compiled by G. Raymond Nunn (1973), xii, 44pp. ISBN 0-89644-533-X.
14. *Indonesian Newspapers: An International Union List*, compiled by G. Raymond Nunn (1973), xv, 131pp. ISBN 0-89644-534-8.
15. *An Annotated Guide to Taiwan Periodical Literature, 1972*, edited by Robert L. Irick (1973), ix, 174pp. ISBN 0-89644-359-0.
16. Yu, Chang-kyun, *Sa-seong Thong-ko* or *Ssu-sheng T'ung-k'ao (A Comprehensive Study of Four Tones)* (1973), xxiv, 286pp. ISBN 0-89644-535-6.
17. Yu, Chang-kyun, *Meng-ku Yün-lüeh (Abbreviated Chinese Rimes in the Mongolian Script)* (1974), xxxiii, 290pp. ISBN 0-89644-536-4.
18. *An Index to Stories of the Supernatural in the* Fa Yüan Chu Lin 法苑珠林

志怪小說引得, compiled by Jordan D. Paper (1973). Paperbound, ix, 29pp. ISBN 0-89644-537-2.

19. *Translation and Permanence in Chinese History and Culture: A Festschrift in Honor of Dr. Hsiao Kung-ch'üan*, edited by David C. Buxbaum and Frederick W. Mote (1973), xxvi, 433pp. ISBN 0-89644-357-4.
20. *An Index to the* Ch'ao-yeh lei-yao 朝野類要引得, compiled by Stephen Hsing-tao Yü (1974), x, 28pp. Paperbound. ISBN 0-89644-538-0.
21. *Neglected Formosa: A Translation from the Dutch of Frederic Coyett's* 't Verwaerloosde Formosa, edited by Inez de Beauclair (1975), xviii, 207pp. ISBN 0-89644-416-3.
22. Day, Clarence Burton, *Peasant Cults in India* (1975), xviii, 126pp. ISBN 0-89644-421-X.
23. Biggerstaff, Knight, *Some Early Chinese Steps Toward Modernization* (1975), vii, 107pp. ISBN 0-89644-417-1.
24. Taylor, Romeyn, *Basic Annals of Ming T'ai-tsu* (1975), vi, 212pp. ISBN 0-89644-433-3.
25. Wang, Sing-wu, *The Organization of Chinese Emigration, 1848-1888* (1978), xviii, 436pp. ISBN 0-89644-480-5.
26. Chiang, Kuei, *The Whirlwind*, translated by Timothy A. Ross (1977), frontis., x, 558pp. ISBN 0-89644-493-7.
27. Ch'en, Ku-ying 陳鼓應, *Lao Tzu: Text, Notes, and Comments*, translated and adapted by Rhett Y.W. Young 楊有維 and Roger T. Ames (1977), viii, 341pp. ISBN 0-89644-520-8.
28. *A Catalog of Kuang-tung Land Records in the Taiwan Branch of the National Central Library*, compiled by Taiwan Branch of the National Central Library, with an introduction by Roy Hofheinze, Jr. (1975), xxvii, 77pp. ISBN 0-89644-439-2.
29. *Studia Asiatica: Essays in Asian Studies in Felicitation of the Seventy-fifth Anniversary of Professor Ch'en Shou-yi*, edited by Laurence G. Thompson (1975), xxvii, 485pp. ISBN 0-89644-476-7.
30. Day, Clarence Burton, *Popular Religion in Pre-Communist China* (1975), viii, 102pp. ISBN 0-89644-422-8.
31. Cohen, Alvin P., *Grammar Notes for Introductory Classical Chinese,* rev. 2nd ed. (1980), (viii), 61pp. ISBN 0-89644-633-6.
32. *A Union List of Chinese Periodicals in Universities and Colleges in Taiwan* 中華民國台灣地區大專院校中期刊聯合目錄, compiled by William Ju 諸家駿 (1976), xvii, 580pp. ISBN 0-89644-539-9.
33. *Papers in Honor of Professor Woodbridge Bingham: A Festschrift for his Seventy-fifth Birthday*, edited by James B. Parsons (1976), xvi, 286pp. ISBN 0-89644-466-X.
34. *Concordances and Indexes to Chinese Texts*, compiled by D. L. McMullen (1975), x, 204pp. ISBN 0-89644-427-9.
35. Shih, Shu-ch'ing, *The Barren Years and Other Short Stories and Plays* (1976), vii, 255pp. ISBN 0-89644-473-2.
36. Day, Clarence Burton, *The Indian Interlude* (1977), x, 151pp. 16 pages of photos. ISBN 0-89644-500-3.

37. Day, Clarence Burton, *The Birth Pangs of Pakistan* (1977), viii, 141pp. ISBN 0-89644-498-8.
38. Donner, Frederick W., Jr., comp., *A Preliminary Glossary of Chinese Linguistic Terminology* (1977), x, 117p. ISBN 0-89644-521-6.
39. Reinecke, John E., *Feigned Necessity: Hawaii's Attempt to Obtain Chinese Contract Labor, 1921-1923* (1979), xviii, 697pp. ISBN 0-89644-572-0.
40. Gates, Alan Frederick, *Christianity and Animism in Taiwan* (1979), x, 262pp., 4 photos., 3 fig. ISBN 0-89644-573-9.
41. Crump, J. I., tr., *Chan-Kuo Ts'e*, 2nd ed. Revised (1979), xlii, 641pp. ISBN 0-89644-583-6.

by Thomas P. Nielson (1976), lxxii, 220pp. ISBN 0-89644-553-4.

15. *An Index to Sung Dynasty Titles Extant in* Ts'ung-shu 叢書索引宋文子目, compiled by Brian E. McKnight (1977), xii, 373pp. ISBN 0-89644-554-2.

16. *An Annotated Guide to Documents on Sino-Japanese-Korean Relations in the Late Ch'ing Dynasty* 淸季中日韓關係資料卅種綜合分類目類, compiled by Li Yü-shu 李毓澍 (1977), 2 vols., xxxii, 1-699pp. + xxxii, 701-1, 169pp. ISBN 0-89644-555-0.

17. *Modern Japanese Authors in Area Studies: A Namelist*, compiled by Austin C. W. Shu (1978), xii, 151pp. ISBN 0-89644-517-8.

IN PREPARATION

"A Index to Diplomatic Documents of the Late Ch'ing Dynasty (1875-1911) 淸季外交史料引得," compiled by Robert L. Irick 艾文博.

"Index to Chinese Terms in the English Translations of Henry Doré, *Researches into Chinese Superstitions*, vols. 1-10 and 13," compiled by Anne S. Goodrich.

"Chinese Names of Foreigners in China," edited by Robert L. Irick 艾文溥 and Linda Marks.

"Taiwan Publications, 1964-1974: An Index by Subject, Author, and Title to New Works and Reprints appearing in CMRASC Booklists," edited by Robert L. Irick.

CHINESE MATERIALS AND RESEARCH AIDS SERVICE CENTER

RESEARCH AIDS SERIES

Robert L. Irick, General Editor

1. *A Classified Index to Articles on Fiscal Policy (1945-65)* 財政論文分類索引, compiled by Frank K. S. Yüan 袁坤祥 and Ma Ching-hsien 馬景賢 (1967), xxxvi, 303pp. ISBN 0-89644-540-2.
2. *A Classified Index to Articles on Economics (1945-65)* 經濟論文分類索引, compiled by Frank K. S. Yüan 袁坤賢 and Ma Ching-hsien 馬景賢 (1967), 2 vols., ciii, (1), 1-792pp. + iii, (1), 793-1, 742pp. ISBN 0-89644-541-0.
3. *A Classified Index to Articles on Money and Banking (1945-65)* 貨幣金融論文分類索引, compiled by Frank K. S. Yüan 袁坤祥 and Ma Ching-hsien 馬景賢 (1967), xliii, 329pp. ISBN 0-89644-542-9.
4. *A Concordance to the Poems of Li Ho (790-816)* 李賀詩引得, compiled by Robert L. Irick 艾文博 (1969), xlii, 217pp. ISBN 0-89644-543-7.
5. *A Chinese-Mongolian Dictionary* 漢蒙字典, compiled by Harnod Hakanchulu 哈勘楚倫 (1969), lxxviii, 1,536pp. ISBN 0-89644-544-5.
6. *A Typeset Edition of the Diary of Weng T'ung-ho with Index* 翁同龢日記排印本附索引, edited by Chao Chung-fu 趙中孚 (1970). Text in 5 vols., 5, 1-524pp. + 525-993pp. + 995-1,522pp. + 1,523-2,002pp. + 2,003-2,448pp. Vol. 6: Index (1979), (xxvii), 400p. ISBN 0-89644-545-3.
7. *Title and Author Index to* Ts'ung-shu *in Taiwan Libraries* 臺灣各圖書館現存叢書子目索引, compiled by Wang Pao-hsien 王寶先. Part I: Title Index, 2 vols. (1976), xxi, 868pp. + ii, 740pp. Part II: Author Index (1977), xii, 190pp. ISBN 0-89644-546-1
8. *A Typeset Edition of the* Tu-li ts'un-i 讀例存疑重刊本, edited by Huang Tsing-chia 黃靜嘉 (1970), 5 vols., 1-262pp. + 4, 1-372pp. + 2, 373-699pp. +2, 701-1,025pp. + 2, 1,027-1,357pp. ISBN 0-89644-547-X.
9. *A Concordance to the* Kuan-tzu 管子引得, compiled by Wallace Johnson 莊爲斯 (1970), lxxviii, 1,188pp. ISBN 0-89644-548-8.
10. *Index to the Ho Collection of Twenty-Eight* Shih-hua 索引本何氏歷代詩話, compiled by Helmut Martin 馬漢茂 (1973), 2 vols.: vol. 1, xviii, 533pp.; vol. 2, 1, 860pp. ISBN 0-89644-549-6.
11. *A Concordance to the* Kuo-yü 國語引得, compiled by Wolfgang Bauer 包吾剛 (1973), 2 vols.: vol. 1, xlii, 808pp.; vol. 2, iv, 486pp. ISBN 0-89644-550-X.
12. *A Concordance to the* Jen-wu Chih *with a Text* 人物志引得, compiled by Wolfgang Bauer 包吾剛 (1974), xvi, 240pp. ISBN 0-89644-551-8.
13. *A Concordance to* Han-fei Tzu 韓非子引得, compiled by Wallace Johnson 莊爲斯 (1975), xxxix, 978pp. ISBN 0-89644-552-6.
14. *A Concordance to the Poems of Wei Ying-wu* 韋應物詩注引得, compiled